# I THOUGHT

# SCOUT UNIFORMS

## WERE

# FIREPROOF

### PUTTING THE FUN IN SCOUTING

## Check out these other popular books for youth by Shane Barker!

*Youth Leading Youth*
*Magnifying Your Aaronic Priesthood Calling*
*Even the Prophet Started out as a Deacon*
*Stepping Up, Taking Charge, and Leading the Way*

# I THOUGHT ❧ SCOUT UNIFORMS ❧ WERE FIREPROOF

## PUTTING THE FUN IN SCOUTING

### SHANE BARKER

BONNEVILLE BOOKS
SPRINGVILLE, UTAH

ISBN 13: 978-1-59955-524-9

Published by Bonneville Books, an imprint of Cedar Fort, Inc., 2373 W. 700 S., Springville, UT 84663
Distributed by Cedar Fort, Inc., www.cedarfort.com

LIBRARY OF CONGRESS CATALOGING-IN-PUBLICATION DATA

Barker, Shane R. author.
  I thought Scout uniforms were fireproof! : putting the fun in scouting Shane Barker.
    pages cm
  ISBN 978-1-59955-524-9
  1. Boy Scouts--Recreation. 2. Youth--Recreation. I. Title.

  HS3312.B348 2011
  369.430973--dc22

  2010050864

Cover design by Danie Romrell
Illustrated by Dave Bowman
Cover design © 2011 by Lyle Mortimer
Edited and typeset by Megan E. Welton

Printed in the United States of America

10  9  8  7  6  5  4  3  2  1

Printed on acid-free paper

To Weston

# CONTENTS

# I THOUGHT SCOUT UNIFORMS WERE
# FIREPROOF!

## PUTTING THE FUN IN SCOUTING

Kyle Rogers was puffing for breath as he charged through the brush toward a knotted Ponderosa Pine. He looked back over his shoulder as Michael Swenson and Jeff Anderson raced through the forest behind him.

"Hurry!" he shouted. "We've almost got it!"

Flicking on his flashlight, he began flashing the beam around in all directions.

As soon as they arrived, Michael and Jeff did the same.

"See 'em?"

Kyle shook his head. "Not yet. There's too many trees . . . no, wait! Over there!"

Off in the trees, about forty yards away, a pair of eyes reflected eerily in the beams of their flashlights. With whoops of excitement, the boys dashed toward them.

A little out of breath myself (keeping up with twelve- and thirteen-year-old boys on a mission isn't a leisurely endeavor!) I followed them through the trees. This was our third night at Thunder Ridge Scout Camp, and the boys were racing through a course called the Wolf-eye Trail.

Strips of reflective tape cut into the shapes of eyes had been placed throughout the forest, and the boys were being timed on how fast they could find them all. Spotting a pair of "eyes," the boys would race toward them, flash their lights around until they spotted the next pair, then dash off again. Some of the eyes had been placed high in the trees, some low to the ground, and one pair had even been placed inside a hole in a rotting log.

It was an exciting, challenging event, and the only problem was that there was also an eerie quality in the air that night. The sensation of being watched—or followed—persisted as we raced along. It made the hair prickle on the back of my neck, and I had the disturbing sensation that something was stalking us. It didn't help that Kyle—the troop storyteller—had regaled us the night before with harrowing stories of Bigfoot, the legendary creature with whom he seemed to have a personal acquaintance.

Kyle, Michael, and Jeff were each aware of the eerie atmosphere too, and despite their excitement, I occasionally caught them casting nervous glances over their shoulders as they raced through the forest.

As we approached the halfway point, Michael spotted a pair of especially creepy-looking eyes. The boys were charging toward them when the eyes abruptly blinked . . . and then blinked again . . . and then disappeared as whatever they were attached to skulked away through the trees.

The next instant, the three Scouts raced down the mountain like Olympic sprinters going for the gold—arms and legs spinning like windmills gone mad—leaving me completely alone in the forest and without a flashlight. Kyle later told everyone that he was going ninety miles an hour as he blazed down the mountain, but he was exaggerating.

I know because I passed him, and *I* was only going eighty-five.

I remember another time when our troop was camping along the shore of a small mountain lake. We had an adrenaline-charged boy in the troop named Coleman, who was a nonstop flurry of moving arms and legs. He had more energy than any boy I've ever known, as well as a warm, happy smile that never seemed to leave his face. Coleman was a human firecracker, and his zany, happy-go-lucky personality made every meeting, hike, and campout more exciting just because he was along. He had the ability to make people feel good just by being in the same room with them.

Coleman was also the troop's best fire builder. Even on wet, rainy days—even when the firewood was soaked to the core—he could coax a crackling, snapping fire into life faster than a gifted arsonist with a blowtorch. And he was never without a pocketful of wooden, strike-anywhere matches.

At any rate, the boys were on their way to fish one afternoon, and Coleman was momentarily left behind. Gear flew through the air as he searched his tent for a pair of sunglasses, then he tore off after his friends.

"Hey!" he called. "Wait for me!"

With the frantic desperation of a boy fleeing Bigfoot, Coleman raced down the hill, abruptly tripping over the root of a tree. As he tumbled head-over-heels, a match head apparently ground against the lining of his pocket and flared to life. The burning match ignited another, and then the whole pocketful went up in a small fireball.

Coleman leaped to his feet and began howling like a wildman, jumping and dancing and flapping his arms like a baby bird that's taken a premature step from the nest.

It took several seconds for Coleman to get the fire out, and then he stopped and gaped at the scorched hole in his Scout shorts. He gawked incredulously for a moment, then looked up with an expression of disbelief.

"Hey!" he said. "I thought Scout uniforms were supposed to be fireproof!"

I've always loved those stories. Kyle, Michael, Jeff, and Coleman are four of the finest young men I've ever known, and remembering their adventures reminds me why I enjoy Scouting so much.

More than that, it reminds me that Scouting is *fun!* It's exciting! And any leader called to serve as a Scoutmaster, den mother, or team committee chairman truly has one of the best jobs in the world.

Now you're probably reading this book because you're a Scoutmaster. Or perhaps you're a Varsity team coach, an Explorer post advisor, or a den mother. If that's the case, then you have one of the most exciting leadership positions in the Church. You have the chance to work and spend time with some of the Lord's finest young people. You have the opportunity to work with young men at the age when they're most impressionable . . . and you can have a great time while you're doing it.

And make no mistake—you are in a position to make a tremendous difference in their lives.

One of my favorite Old Testament stories is the tale of David and Goliath. As I'm sure you remember, Goliath was a giant who stood more than eight feet tall. Carrying enormous weapons and girded about with armor, he must have looked terrifying to young David—absolutely terrifying!

Nevertheless, David went out to fight the giant alone

and without armor or protection, taking nothing with him but a simple slingshot and a few small stones.

You already know what happened: David faced the giant—and slew him.

The scriptures don't tell us where David learned to use his slingshot. But today that's exactly the sort of thing a boy might learn in Scouting. As a Scout leader, you're teaching boys to use tools they need to face the Goliaths in their lives. And I just can't think of a more important job anywhere.

The only problem is that your program has to compete with sports, school, and—if you are an Explorer advisor—jobs and girls. It isn't always easy. But if you can create a program full of fun and adventure, if you can give the boys thrills and excitement to complement the time they spend in school, the battle's over.

And that's what this book is about. It's about taking the meetings, merit badges, and skills that make up the Scouting program and pumping them full of fun. It's about making them exciting and compelling, giving you the chance to teach your boys to use their slingshots.

Are you ready?

Great! Then I have a few ideas to help you out. The list is by no means comprehensive, but it should give you enough ideas and insight to put you on a collision course with exciting Scouting adventures.

So let's get going!

I know you're going to have as much fun as I've had!

# HOW TO GET STARTED!

 **Remember that Scouting is more than troop meetings, flag ceremonies, and merit badges.** Start looking for the fun—and the excitement!—in your upcoming activities.

 **Go ahead and start reading.** You can read the book from beginning to end, or you can skip ahead to those chapters that best meet your immediate needs. This book is written specifically for the leaders of Boy Scouts, but it will be helpful to the leaders of older Scouts and younger Scouts too.

 **Give the ideas a try!** Really! A few of them might mean taking a step or two outside your personal comfort zone (like wearing an official uniform or singing a patrol song), but give 'em a try! Give these ideas a chance to energize your program!

# 1

# PANCAKES, GUMBO, AND DUTCH-OVEN PIZZA

## PUTTING THE FUN IN COOKING

Thirteen-year-old David Hardman placed his hand over the grill to check the heat, then checked his stopwatch.

"Are you ready?"

Tyler Jellen took a moment to make certain he had everything positioned just where he wanted it, then nodded.

"Ready."

"Okay, then. On your mark . . . get set . . . *go!*"

Tyler quickly poured circles of batter onto the grill as the troop cheered him on. He poured until the entire grill was covered, waited a brief moment, then grabbed a spatula and began flipping the golden pancakes.

David looked up from his stopwatch.

"A minute thirty, Tyler! Keep going! You're doing great!"

Tyler tapped his foot impatiently as he waited for the pancakes to brown—he knew he'd lose points if they were too doughy—then he scooped the fluffy cakes off the grill and onto a waiting platter. The next instant, he was pouring more batter onto the grill.

"All right, Tyler!" someone shouted. "You're doing great! Keep going!"

With the intensity of a surgeon, Tyler again began flipping pancakes, letting them fry just long enough to turn a golden brown before scooping them from the grill. He was going so fast that once—in his excitement—he missed the platter and sent a pancake flying into the dirt. He shook his head in frustration, prompting a chorus of support from his audience.

"Don't worry about it, Tyler!"

"You're doing great, Ty! Keep going!"

"Come on, Tyler, you've almost got it!"

Tyler flipped the last of the pancakes onto the platter and was working on his third batch when David looked up from his watch.

"Ten more seconds, Tyler!" he shouted. "Five . . . four . . . three . . . two . . . one . . . STOP!"

Tyler wiped his hands on his apron—which was patterned in camouflage with the words "Grill Sergeant" printed across the front—and looked around.

"Who counted?" he asked. "How many did I get?"

"Twenty-six," someone answered. "You missed the record by four."

Tyler rolled his eyes. "That's all? Twenty-six? Man, I was *sure* I had it this time!"

I grinned as I watched. And so did everyone else. On the troop's last campout, a Scout named Kevin set the troop record by cooking up thirty pancakes in ten minutes, and Tyler had vowed to beat him. He didn't quite make it, but his energetic attempt made almost enough pancakes to feed the entire troop, and he'd turned a normally dull chore into an adventure for the whole troop.

Most Scouts don't list cooking among the activities they most look forward to when they go camping. After all, most boys go into the mountains to hike and swim and fish. And the more time they spend in their backcountry kitchens—building fires, preparing meals, or washing pots and pans—the less time they have for more adventurous activities.

But cooking is a skill that Scouts can use every day of their lives. It's a skill that will serve them throughout their teenage years, on their missions, away at college, and all of their adult lives too. So a Scoutmaster who can bring out the adventure of cooking while developing the boys' skills will truly be doing his troop a service.

Besides, cooking can be fun! And when spiced with a little mountain air and a touch of wood smoke flavoring, even the most ordinary meals can turn a backcountry outing into a rousing adventure.

When I was in college, I served as an assistant to a Scoutmaster named Roy Harris, who truly knew how to make Boy Scout cooking fun. On one campout he asked each Scout to bring one can of food—any kind of food at all—to contribute to the troop dinner. Upon arrival at the campsite, Roy collected these cans and divided them into two categories: fruit . . . and everything else. He assigned me to take the fruit and make two peach-pear-pineapple cobblers.

Harris then asked his senior patrol leader to divide the remaining cans—chilies, stews, refried beans, corns, string beans, and other various items—equally between the troop's two patrols. He then took a large pot and announced, "You have been stranded in the mountains without knives, can openers, or tools of any kind. But you need to eat, so you need to get these cans opened. The first patrol to open its cans and get the contents into this pot will not have to wash any of the dinner dishes tonight. Everyone understand? Okay, then . . . ready . . . *go!*"

The Scouts stood uncertainly for a moment, then jumped as a boy named Jeff took a rock and smashed his can with enough force that green beans exploded through the air like shrapnel from a hand grenade.

Scoutmaster Harris calmly pulled a bean from his hair and shook his head. "It goes without saying," he said, "that the cans will be disqualified unless their contents are still edible."

With that, the rival patrols separated and began work on their cans. One boy opened his by hammering his belt buckle through the top. Another gave his can a hard wallop along the edge with a hard rock, splitting it neatly open.

I never did see how the boys in the other patrol opened their cans—and they refused to tell, saying their secret would come in handy the next time we tried the activity— but they managed to win the contest by several minutes.

When the competition was over, the cans were all dumped into a single pot and stirred together over a snapping fire. The resulting conglomeration was ghastly to look at (I won't even attempt to describe it!), but it tasted great! More than that, the activity took the work out of making dinner and turned it into a game.

Harris had other ideas for making cooking adventurous. He usually had each patrol plan and cook its own meals on campouts, but before anyone sat down to eat, he and his senior patrol leader judged each patrol's meal. They awarded points for originality, quality, and tastiness, and they ate with the patrol who prepared the best food.

Harris explained that the Scouts considered it an honor to have the Scoutmaster to dinner, but that wasn't the only reason the competition was successful.

"My senior patrol leader and I always made dessert for the winning patrol," he said. "And the losing patrol was expected to clean up after the entire troop."

Harris said that the anticipation of cobbler alone was incentive enough to spur the most unmotivated Scouts into action. Campout meals immediately improved from hot dogs and tinfoil dinners to stroganoff and chicken gumbo. After a little experience, most of the Scouts learned that extravagant, almost exotic meals often required no more work than tinfoil dinners.

On one campout, a Scout named Darren spent only a few minutes with his father in a local supermarket, then surprised the whole troop by transforming a few packages of dry ingredients into beef teriyaki with noodles.

"No need to tell you which patrol I ate with *that* night," Harris said.

Contests have improved the cooking in other troops too. After several nights of Dutch-oven training, one Scoutmaster planned a cooking demonstration in the church parking lot. The Scouts divided themselves into pairs and drew slips of paper for their cooking assignments. Some drew main courses. Others drew vegetables. And some drew desserts.

To make things even more interesting, the troop not only invited the Scouts' parents and bishopric to sample the results but invited the ward Beehive class too.

On the night of the exhibition, guests wandered around and watched the various groups in action. Then, when everything had been cooked, the meal was placed on picnic tables, and everyone was invited to dig in. The bishopric was given the chore of naming the best dish.

Another Scoutmaster encouraged culinary creativity with themed meals. On one campout, he asked his Scouts to cook something western. The next time it was Italian. Then Mexican. On Hawaiian night, his chief chef—a Life Scout named Travis—organized a fun but simple Hawaiian dinner by wrapping chicken breasts in foil with pre-cooked rice and pineapple. He placed these in the glowing coals of the troop campfire for forty-five minutes, and while the chicken cooked, Travis had the Scouts wrap ears of corn in foil with dabs of butter. They cooked these for fifteen minutes. The meal was topped off by instant Hawaiian punch and pineapple pudding.

The meal was no harder to make than tinfoil dinners, but it tasted much better. It was more creative. And it was a lot more fun.

Now, it would be silly to believe that you could implement any of these ideas into your own troop program without a little instruction to the boys. After all, it's a good bet that many of your Scouts have trouble making peanut-butter sandwiches without a little help.

But if you need to teach basic cooking skills, don't lecture! Instead, take the Scouts into the parking lot—or into the foothills—and let them cook! Let them learn firsthand how it's done! Let them experience the fun! Let them discover for themselves the thrill that backcountry cooking can be.

One Scoutmaster took his troop to a local park to demonstrate the differences between freeze-dried and dehydrated foods. Using borrowed propane stoves to cook over, the boys heated up one freeze-dried and one dehydrated meal. The freeze-dried meal was ready to eat five minutes after the water boiled, while the dehydrated dinner required nearly twenty-five minutes of simmering.

After both meals were ready, the Scoutmaster had a few questions.

"Which meal cooked fastest?"

Everyone answered together. "Freeze-dried!"

"Right. So, on a backpacking trip where you're cooking over stoves and you have to carry all of your fuel, which meal would be better?"

"Freeze-dried!"

"Right again. But freeze-dried food is a lot more expensive than dehydrated food. So if you're cooking over a wood fire and don't need to buy or carry your fuel, which meal do you suppose would be better?"

"Dehydrated!"

The boys not only learned firsthand how to cook the stuff, but they learned valuable information too.

Matt Dixon, a Scoutmaster I met at summer camp, sparked his troop's imagination when he showed them all the things they could do with a Boy Scout mess kit.

"Almost everyone has an official Boy Scout mess kit," he told me. "The boys get them on their birthdays, and they get them for Christmas. But I've only known a handful of Scouts who really knew how to use them."

So, taking his troop to a nearby park, Dixon opened up a mess kit and laid out all the parts. He had a quart-sized pot with a lid, a combination measuring drinking cup, and two frying pans that doubled as plates. The boys then spent the next hour or so experimenting with all the different things they could do with them. Cooking over a couple of backpacking stoves, they fried, baked, boiled, simmered, mixed, and finally washed their dishes . . . all with nothing more than the equipment contained in their mess kits.

"Now," he said after he'd finished. "We're going to meet here again next week. And I'll give prizes to the Scouts who cook the tastiest, most creative dishes with nothing but their mess kits."

The next week, most of the boys cooked up desserts of one kind or another. But the winning chef was a Scout who used his cook pot as a Dutch oven—placing charcoal briquettes above and below—and cooked a pizza in it.

No chapter on Boy Scout cooking would ever be complete without a few words about primitive or utensil-less cooking—especially if you're like the hundreds of Scouters who hate a lot of messy preparation and cleanup!

Primitive cooking is a fantastic way to interject adventure into a backcountry dinner. It's different enough that most Scouts enjoy it. And the nice thing is that entire meals—including soups, drinks, main courses, and desserts—can be made without using a single utensil.

During a Boy Leader Training Course (called "Timberline" in my council), an assistant Scoutmaster named Jameson conducted one of the most fascinating primitive cooking demonstrations I have ever witnessed. He took the Scouts deep into the woods to a primitive campsite he had constructed to resemble something out of *The Swiss Family Robinson*. Near the trees, he had a chair made out of rope. In the clearing, he had a sundial made out of short sticks.

And near his fireplace, he had a table and benches made out of logs.

After taking the Scouts on a quick tour of his campsite, Jameson began cooking his primitive dinner. He slapped hamburger patties onto flat rocks near the fire, tossed pork chops directly onto the bed of glowing coals, boiled soup in a paper cup, cooked bacon in a paper bag, fried an egg on a stick, and baked a cake in an orange peel.

Later on, back in camp, the Scouts were given the same foods Jameson had used in his demonstration but no utensils. But that didn't matter. Jameson had taught his lesson well enough that the hungry Scouts were all anxious to give it a try.

On a campout in the red rock country of Southern Utah, a Scoutmaster named Nick Anderson made primitive cooking adventurous by organizing a "caveman" dinner.

His Scouts all wrinkled their noses when they heard about it.

"What's a 'caveman' dinner?" someone asked.

"Just an ordinary meal," Anderson said. "Except that you have to *make* all of your own utensils."

The Scouts were instantly enthusiastic. They quickly set about carving their own forks, spoons, plates, and bowls. One Scout whittled a fork large enough to pitch hay, and another carved an elegant piece that had a fork on one end and a spoon on the other. The troop's favorite, though, was a bowl that *looked* wonderful but leaked all over its owner's lap, delighting everyone.

During another Timberline course, Scoutmaster Rick Harward put fun into breakfast one morning with a treasure hunt. He gave each patrol a card with directions to "check beneath the camp flagpole," or "look behind your patrol leader's tent," and so on. In each spot, he had placed an ingredient or utensil necessary for cooking French toast.

Within minutes, Scouts were dashing around the camp, collecting materials. And the first patrol to actually finish their breakfast was given bowls of strawberries for dessert.

I've always liked pancakes on campouts because there are so many fun things you can do with them. One Scout-master—giving his Scouts a couple of days' notice before the campout and assigning them to cook in pairs—gave awards to the boys who cooked their pancakes with the most original filling. One pair used fresh strawberries. Another used bananas and a third pair used peaches. One team even used peanut butter and ice cream.

The Scoutmaster ensured good cooking by awarding extra points for taste, appearance, and quality.

The nice thing about activities like these is that they make cooking fun and adventurous. Instead of being a chore that no one wants to volunteer for, cooking suddenly becomes a game that everyone wants to join in.

Moreover, games help to stir the boys' imaginations. They improve the Scouts' skill and confidence around the kitchen.

Cooking is one of the most practical skills many boys ever learn in Scouting. It's one of the few skills they can put into use every day. And if you can teach your Scouts the simple skills they need to prepare a good meal, you will have truly done them a valuable service.

So make cooking a vital part of your troop program. Encourage creativity and originality, and give the boys the opportunity to experiment. Get ready to have fun . . . and probably gain a few pounds along the way!

## HOW TO GET STARTED!

 **Don't fall into the trap** of doing all of the cooking on your next Scout campout. Learning to cook for others—not to mention learning to plan and purchase the ingredients to make a meal—is too valuable a skill to deprive your Scouts of. Instead, look for ways to turn cooking into an adventure rather than a chore.

 **Start planning for your next campout now.** Try choosing a themed meal like western, Italian, or Mexican to spark the boys' imagination and creativity.

 **Use the spirit of competition** to get your Scouts thinking "outside the box." If you have more than one patrol, offer to make dessert for the patrol with the tastiest, most creative meal.

 **Find ways to let the boys experiment.** Start with simple cooking lessons over charcoal briquettes at the local park or over small fires (regulations permitting!) in the foothills.

 **For a change of pace**—and to help prepare Scouts for trips where fires are not permitted—teach the boys to prepare meals that don't require any cooking.

 **Check the library**—or the Internet—for books on primitive cooking for more ideas.

# 2

# WHO FORGOT THEIR
# NECKERCHIEF?

## PUTTING THE FUN IN UNIFORMS

**N**athan Brooks, the thirteen-year-old senior patrol leader, grinned mischievously. Standing in front of the troop, he held a clipboard, preparing to conduct uniform inspection. His grin widened a fraction.

The interesting thing was that everyone else was grinning too. The Scouts all knew that Nathan was about to inspect their uniforms, but in this troop, uniform inspection was something everyone looked forward to.

Nathan, meanwhile, was drawing out the suspense, hoping to make things as dramatic as possible. He hummed and hawed over trivial business until he knew the troop couldn't stand it anymore, then finally cleared his throat.

"All right, you all look sharp tonight," he said, looking everyone up and down. "So let's get down to business."

He reached into an envelope, drew out a slip of paper, and grinned again.

"Tonight we're going to award patrol points"—he paused to heighten the effect—"to everyone . . . wearing . . . Scout socks!"

The Scouts immediately began checking one another's legs. Almost everyone was wearing Scout shorts that night, and most of the boys were wearing official Scout socks. Two boys, though, were wearing white athletic socks, and one Scout wasn't wearing any socks at all.

"I *knew* it was going to be socks!" the last Scout wailed. "I couldn't find mine tonight!"

Nathan took a few minutes to count and record the results of his inspection on his clipboard.

"Okay," he said finally. "The Frogs have four guys with official socks, and the Seals have three. The Frogs win the spirit stick for the week."

The Frogs cheered and took possession of an old broomstick decorated to look like an Indian spear. They looked as excited as boys who had just won the Little League World Series.

"Winning that old stick is a mark of honor in my troop," said Roy Harris, the troop Scoutmaster. "And it all revolves around Nathan's inspections."

Harris said that uniform inspection was one of the most popular elements of his weekly troop meetings, and he explained how it worked.

"Every night, Nathan selects one part of the Scout uniform and gives points for every Scout who is wearing it correctly. The winning patrol wins the spirit stick for the week, and as soon as a patrol wins it a total of six times, they earn a movie night."

Harris explained that what made Nathan's inspections so successful was that no one ever knew exactly what part of the uniform he was going to choose. One night it was neckerchiefs. Another time it was patrol patches. Other times it's been belts, epaulets, troop numerals, or hats. And—because this was a by-the-book troop—he once even gave points to every Scout who had a quarter for emergency phone calls in his pocket.

"One night he even checked for official buttons on everyone's shirts," Harris said.

Wearing a uniform was such fun in Harris's troop that Scouts not only wore them to troop meetings but on hikes and campouts too. More than that, neither Harris nor his assistants ever had to remind anyone. They had developed such a keen, productive rivalry between the troop's patrols that the Scouts wouldn't have *dreamed* of attending a troop activity without their uniforms.

Many boys don't like wearing Scout uniforms. They often feel self-conscious about wearing them in public, and it's often difficult to get them to wear uniforms to meetings, let alone on hikes and campouts. And many boys lack the money or motivation to buy uniforms.

But uniforming is one of the eight methods used by the Boy Scouts of America to promote character, citizenship, and personal fitness. That's because uniforms not only instill a sense of pride and belonging within the boys who wear them, but they help to build troop spirit too. They help *you* to achieve your goals as Scoutmaster.

Uniforms can also do wonderful things for the pride of the troop and the self-esteem of the boys. That's because when they are all clad in identical uniforms, they look sharp. And that sets them apart from other units. It makes them feel good.

At summer camp one year, I worked with a troop that showed up to flag ceremony each morning in flawless uniforms. Not only that, but the boys stood in sharp, straight lines, complete with troop and patrol flags. And even those boys who had to be goaded into wearing their uniforms loved the attention they received. The camp staff *oohed* and *aahed* over them. And other troops watched them enviously through the corners of their eyes.

"We looked *so* good!" one of the boys told me. "I felt sorry for those troops that didn't have uniforms."

There's no question that uniforms can spark magic and excitement in your troop program. They can be the catalyst that transforms an ordinary, run-of-the-mill troop into a compelling, spirited unit.

The biggest problem is just getting started.

One troop solved the problem with a bead program. Each Scout was given a leather cord that he wore looped around his collar. Then, he was given beads as recognition for participating in hikes, campouts, and other activities. Different colors of beads represented different activities.

"The Scouts were constantly trying to earn more beads," Scoutmaster Robert Walker explained. "Especially the younger ones. They saw the older boys with twenty or thirty beads and were anxious to catch up. So when we had trouble getting the boys out in uniform, we added that to our program."

Walker explained that after wearing a complete uniform to four consecutive meetings, the boys were given a red bead. In addition, a bronze bead was awarded for wearing the uniform on a hike or campout.

Scoutmaster Alex Marshall put excitement into uniforming with the help of Marty, his senior patrol leader, who came to each troop meeting with one part of his uniform on incorrectly. He sometimes wore an ordinary belt, for instance, or white socks. Some nights he placed patches on the wrong pockets or wore his neckerchief inside out. He gave a candy bar to the first Scout to identify what was wrong.

Another Scoutmaster had a similar idea. To help his Scouts better understand proper uniforming, he occasionally dressed up one of the Scouts as improperly as possible. He sewed patches on the wrong sleeves, tucked pant legs inside socks, unbuttoned buttons, and so on. And he often included many subtle mistakes such as skipping loops with the belt.

Then, during troop meeting, he had "Tommy Tenderfoot" give a short speech in front of the troop and then leave the room. Each patrol then tried to identify from memory as many uniform mistakes as possible. This not only created a fun competition, but it also generated several interesting discussions.

"Sometimes the boys disagreed over some point, such as whether a certain patch or badge was being worn correctly," the leader told me. "So we'd talk about it for a few minutes and then look it up in the Scout Handbook."

Many troops put fun into their uniforms by personalizing them. Some, for instance, make their own neckerchiefs. This gives the boys a sense of ownership, makes the neckerchiefs more fun to wear, and sets the troop apart at camporees and other events where other troops are present.

Having custom-made patrol patches is a similar idea. When I was an assistant Scoutmaster, we had a group of Scouts who called themselves the Frog Patrol. The only problem was that they didn't like the frog patrol patch offered by the BSA. So with the help of their mothers, they bought blank patches and sewed their own frogs on. The patches were so striking that people noticed them everywhere they went. And the boys loved it. People were constantly asking where they'd gotten their patches. That attention alone was enough motivation that the boys were certain to wear their uniforms everywhere they went.

Many troops identify themselves with distinctive "Class B" uniforms, which generally consist of custom-made T-shirts worn over official Scout shorts or pants. Modern silk-screening techniques allow troops to inexpensively design and create their own T-shirts, which the boys are likely to wear even when they're *not* involved in Scout activities.

(While you're being creative, remember to stay within official guidelines. One time a group of volunteers inappropriately voted to make Scout shirts and blue jeans the official uniform of their entire district.)

One troop managed to get all the boys in uniform but then had trouble getting them excited about wearing neckerchiefs. So once a month, as part of their opening ceremony, they began giving awards for the most original neckerchief slides. (It's funny, but many Scouts who don't like neckerchiefs do like the slides!)

At any rate, neckerchiefs ceased being a problem. Scouts soon wore them every week. Not only that, but they also wore them with the most outlandish slides ever created. Some boys wore slides they made with plaster or carved out of wood. (One Scout carved an intricate pair of hiking boots, then cut a notch into them every time he went on a hike.) It made the whole experience more fun.

Once uniforms become a tradition in your troop, the hard part is over. New Scouts coming into the troop will want to look like their older friends. But establishing that tradition continues to be one of the toughest things in any troop.

One Scoutmaster, on his first night with a new troop, showed up to Scout meeting dressed in full uniform. He had enough patches, beads, and badges that he looked like an admiral with seventy years' experience.

His Scouts—most of them dressed in T-shirts and blue jeans—looked at him in awe. He noticed their wonder and said, "I will never tell you that you have to wear your uniforms. But if you really want to look sharp, if you really want to have fun in Scouting, you'll start wearing them."

And it worked. Little by little—and one by one—the boys began showing up in uniform.

If you want the magic of uniforms sparking life into your troop, be sure that you set the proper example. Make certain that you have a full uniform with all of the correct insignia. Moreover, make sure that your assistants are similarly prepared.

Next, work on your senior patrol leader. After all, he's the one the boys should be following. Get him on board, and half the battle will be over. Then go to work on your patrol leaders. With this core of adult and boy leaders coming to meetings in uniform, it will be difficult for the rest of the troop not to follow suit.

It also helps to start a "storehouse" of used uniform parts. When a Scout grows out of a shirt or pair of pants— or when he leaves the troop—ask him to donate his used uniform to the troop. These "experienced" uniforms can then be given to Scouts who may not be able to afford one. (Some troops even buy uniforms from graduating Scouts, selling them to younger boys at reduced prices.)

By wearing their uniforms, your Scouts will feel a healthy

sense of belonging. And that's good for them. They'll feel pride that many of them can't get anywhere else. They'll develop a better self-image. In addition, they'll be constantly reminded of the principles they stand for as Boy Scouts.

Uniforms themselves will not automatically turn your boys into fantastic Scouts. But once you establish a tradition of uniforming in your troop, you'll find the Scouts more eager to attend meetings. They'll feel more purpose and spirit as a team. They'll feel better about themselves.

And all those things together add up to one thing: fun!

## HOW TO GET STARTED:

- **Give the boys incentives** for wearing their uniforms. If the Scouts have a *reason* to wear their uniforms, they'll be more likely to *want* to.

- **Teach your Scouts how to wear their uniforms correctly.** The more they know about the uniform and the reasons behind it, the more they understand the importance of wearing their uniform and the more likely they'll be to buy into the program.

- **If you want your Scouts to wear uniforms,** first let them know that you expect it. More than that, lead the way by wearing a complete uniform yourself. Make certain that it fits correctly and that you have the appropriate patches and insignia.

- **Find ways to provide uniforms** for those Scouts who may not be able to purchase one. Establish a storehouse of used uniform parts, and collect experienced uniforms from growing Scouts.

# 3

# THE PILOT LIGHT'S OUT ON THE
# NUCLEAR REACTOR!

## PUTTING THE FUN IN MEETINGS

**C**ade Wilson speared a hotdog with a green willow branch.

"So let me get this straight," he said, furrowing his brow like a mathematician fretting over a knotty equation. "You get your paycheck, but you don't get all of the money?"

"Not all of it, no," Scoutmaster Will Wright said. "Your employer will automatically deduct state and federal taxes—"

"No way!"

"—not to mention Social Security, retirement, union dues, possibly—"

"You're kidding!" a boy named Ben said, talking

through a mouthful of roasted hotdog. "How much does that all come to?"

"Well, it differs from person to person," Wright said casually. "But in my case, it usually comes to about thirty percent."

"Thirty percent?! I don't believe it!"

"Believe it. For every hundred dollars I earn, I only get about—"

"Seventy?"

Wright nodded again. "About that."

Cade shook his head. "But that's not fair! It's *your* money!"

"Well, yes . . . but without taxes, how do you think the government could pay for highways? Or policemen? Or firemen?"

The Scouts were all quiet as they pondered Wright's question. They'd all heard about taxes in general terms before, but until now—as they roasted hotdogs in the glow of a bright, snapping campfire—taxes had never been anything more than a remote, obscure concept that might or might not someday actually affect them.

The troop was working on the Citizenship in the World Merit Badge. Scoutmaster Wright had wanted to lead a discussion on the rights and duties of citizens and had begun a discussion on taxes, knowing that it would generate a lively debate.

But wanting to avoid a classroom-like atmosphere, he also decided to conduct the meeting in the local foothills, around a campfire, as the boys roasted hotdogs.

And it worked. The wilderness setting diminished the school-like atmosphere the meeting normally would have had. And by the time they returned home, the boys felt that they'd had an adventure rather than a lesson on citizenship.

The problem with Scout meetings is that they have to compete with so many other activities. Little League, for instance, as well as soccer, football, and lacrosse. And that's on top of all the school plays, band concerts, parties, movies, family outings, and other activities that young men are expected to take part in. So unless you have an exciting, compelling program working for you, attending a troop meeting is likely to be low on your Scouts' priority list.

Moreover, when troop meetings become mundane, routine, and (shudder) predictable, many boys don't think twice about missing them since they can tell you minute-by-minute what's likely to be happening anyway.

The good news is that it's not hard to run an exciting troop meeting. As a matter of fact, you can develop a program that's consistently fun and exciting just by implementing three ingredients: action, variety, and purpose.

How do you do that?

Let's take a look.

## ACTION

If you want your Scouts coming out week after week, don't plan on having them sit and listen to talks and lectures. They get enough of that at school. And the only reason many boys are in Scouts anyway is that it's supposed to be fun.

This doesn't mean that you can't ever have a sit-in-a-circle, take-notes-while-I-write-on-the-blackboard-kind-of lesson. After all, you've got to plan the next campout *sometime*. But if that's all the boys come to expect—if that's all they have to look forward to week after week—they'll go back to playing baseball.

So sandwich your sit-down, please-be-quiet-and-pay-attention-while-I-talk lessons between get-up-and-go-and-make-all-the-noise-you-want activities.

One of the best, most versatile ideas I ever saw for putting action into a troop meeting was a game called Get Out of That. I've seen a couple of troops use it, and it's never failed to inject action and excitement into a meeting while giving the boys the chance to learn or practice good, old-fashioned Scouting skills at the same time.

The game is simple. Divide the troop into patrols, which rotate through the parking lot (or through the Scout room, depending upon the nature of your challenges) to different stations.

Each station then presents some challenge that the patrol has fifteen minutes to solve.

One time, for example, a patrol leader named Scott placed a rope in a corner of the church parking lot so that it made an eight-foot circle. In the center he placed a candle. And to the side he had several poles, various lengths of rope, and a handful of matches.

"This is a nuclear reactor, and the pilot light's gone out," he said, pointing to the candle when the first patrol approached. "You need to light it as fast as you can without stepping inside the circle. And"—he pointed to the ropes and poles—"this is all you have to do it with. Now get out of that!"

After a quick discussion, the Scouts lashed sticks together until they had a single pole long enough to extend a burning match to the candle.

Scott jotted their time on a scorecard as the boys dashed off to the next station.

The nice thing about Get Out of That is that it's so versatile. You can dream up challenges to cover first aid, knots, cooking, or any skill you might want to review. It allows boys opportunities to think, to be creative, and to come up with innovative solutions to problems. And it helps the boys learn to work together, which develops teamwork.

More to the point, the game is fun because it involves action. And the more lively your troop meetings are, the more fun they'll be, and the more success you'll have with them.

I once watched a troop practicing first aid. Small groups of Scouts sat in different corners of the room, the boys taking turns playing the part of the patient.

The Scoutmaster, meanwhile, stood in the center of the room, reading the signs and symptoms of different medical emergencies and watching as each group treated its "patient."

The Scoutmaster and his assistants supervised the action, giving each patrol points according to the quality of their work, then offering feedback and suggestions before going on to the next situation.

What made the activity so compelling was that the boys were all involved—either as patients or rescuers. And rather than lecture the boys on first aid, the Scoutmaster found ways to make his lesson come to life.

You can do the same thing.

## VARIETY

If every football game ended the same way, you'd soon grow tired of watching. You wouldn't need to watch because you'd already know what was going to happen.

But athletic events are exciting because you never know what's going to happen next. Everyone knows the team will try to move the ball, but no one knows exactly how it's going to happen.

And that's the way your troop meetings should be. It's

okay if the Scouts know they're going to be working on the Nature Merit Badge Wednesday night, but you should be unpredictable enough that they don't know exactly how they're going to go about it.

A couple of years ago, I was invited to watch a troop that was working on first aid and emergency preparedness. A couple of days before the meeting, each Scout received a note in the mail that simply read, "Bloody Wednesday's coming . . . be sure you come to Scout meeting!"

A day or two later, bits of cardboard cut into the shape of sabers were delivered to each Scout. On these was an invitation: "Want to see a real cut up? Come to Scout meeting Wednesday night!"

By the night of the meeting, everyone's anticipation level was so high that Scouts wouldn't have dreamed of skipping out. And they weren't disappointed. The Scoutmaster had planned exciting activities that involved both first aid and preparedness skills. And to cap things off—and to meet a merit badge requirement—the boys finished the meeting by taking turns lowering one another off the roof of the church.

But that's not all. Inside the Scout room were signs and posters designed to spark interest in the *next* week's meeting. One said, "If you think things were hot tonight, you won't believe what's going to happen next week!" Another read: "What do broken bones and Jell-O have in common? Be here next week to find out!"

The posters not only generated interest, but they raised the boys' anticipation level. They aroused everyone's curiosity, and that alone was enough to have the boys counting the minutes to the next meeting.

While we're talking about variety, remember that you

don't have to meet the same night and in the same place week after week. Sure, it's easier to remember if you do, but if you have a good phone-calling system, you can get the word out if you ever need to make a change.

So meet outside once in a while! Even if you're simply planning a campout or learning about citizenship, try holding your meeting in a park, up the canyon, or in someone's backyard. (One troop I used to work with met outside all summer long, so when we needed a change of pace we went inside!)

Another troop I was part of only met as a troop on the first and third Wednesdays of the month. On the second and fourth Wednesdays, the Scouts met as patrols under the supervision of assistant Scoutmasters. And whenever the month had a fifth Wednesday, the troop met for games or movie parties.

This simple formula was successful for a couple of reasons. First, alternating troop and patrol nights created a healthy diversity. The troop was able to accomplish its objectives while the boys—who organized and conducted their individual patrol meetings—were able to keep their own projects and programs rolling along as well.

And the movie parties, which occurred two or three times a year, provided a healthy change of pace, as well as something more to look forward to.

There are other things you should consider too. The Scoutmaster's Handbook, for instance, suggests that you have an activity—as opposed to a meeting—once a week. This means that if you have a campout or hike one weekend, you shouldn't feel obligated to have a regular troop meeting too. (Giving the Scouts a night off once in a while creates variety too!)

Finally, if you find a good, fun activity that the boys enjoy, be careful not to wear it out. Even the most exciting games can become old after awhile, so don't overuse your best ones. Find new and different ways to keep things lively.

## PURPOSE

Unless your meetings have specific goals and objectives, your Scouts really have no reason to attend. And even twelve- and thirteen-year-olds are perceptive enough to know when their time is being wasted. So by the time they leave troop meeting, every Scout should believe that he's become more skilled, more knowledgeable, or more prepared in some aspect of his life.

When you begin planning any meeting, the first thing you should do is decide exactly what you want to accomplish. This objective should be real and concrete. You might decide, for instance, that every Scout will pass off requirements five and six of a particular merit badge, or that they will tie the bowline and the timber hitch. Then, once you know exactly what you need to accomplish, you can begin designing activities to get you there.

If your Scouts truly believe that your meetings are helpful, they'll not only be more willing to come, they'll actually be eager for more. They'll realize that Scout meetings are not just another draw on their time. So let them see and chart their own progress.

When my troop signed up for rifle shooting at Thunder Ridge Scout Camp, the instructor put the boys on the rifle range the first day of class and had them shoot a couple of targets. He kept these, and then on the last day of class, he had everyone shoot again. Then he took both targets, stapled them together, and handed them back to the Scouts.

The results were amazing. Targets from the first day

displayed random groups and scattered shots. Targets from the last day had tight, accurate groups and good scores. Whether they actually earned that difficult merit badge or not, every boy had concrete evidence that he had improved his marksmanship.

Another Scoutmaster—before his troop began working on personal fitness—had each Scout record his best number of push-ups, sit-ups, and so on. Then, after each Scout had completed the training and conditioning required by the merit badge, they checked again. Without exception, every Scout had increased his strength, speed, and agility. Each boy had tangible proof that he had improved himself. And even boys who were already accomplished athletes were convinced that troop meetings had helped them to become even stronger and faster.

Don't ever waste your boys' time. Make sure that every time they meet with you they go home better and richer for the experience. And give them chances to measure their progress. If they believe that they're succeeding, they'll not only develop a better self image, but they'll also be coming back for more.

Troop meetings are where you'll spend most of your time with your Scouts. So make them fun and interesting. Find ways to fill your meetings with action and excitement. Fill them with enough variety to keep them fresh and lively. And make certain that every meeting fulfills some purpose and sends the boys away better for having been there.

Your Scouts will not only have more fun, but you'll be surprised at how much fun *you'll* be having too.

# HOW TO GET STARTED!

 **Take a minute to think** about what you have planned for your next troop meeting. Try to think of some way to inject a little action into it.

 **If your troop generally meets indoors,** try conducting your next meeting in a park or in someone's backyard. Even if you're just planning to work on Bookbinding or Library Science, the simple change in scenery will add variety to your program.

 **Whenever you need** to have a sit-in-a-circle-and-listen kind of meeting, be sure to include a game or activity to add a touch of adventure to the evening.

 **Before your next meeting,** be sure to list specific objectives. Make them concrete and measurable. Be sure you know—and be sure your boys know—that they are making progress.

# 4

# HOW TO PACK A
# BACKPACK

## PUTTING THE FUN INTO MERIT BADGES

Todd Rainer pulled a face as he read the card.

"Go directly to jail," he read. "Do not pass Go. Do not collect $200."

The thirteen-year-old Scout mumbled something regrettable beneath his breath, then took the small racecar that marked his spot on the game board and placed it in jail.

"This is my second time!" he complained. "I'm like a jail magnet . . . I never get a break!"

Marty Gates laughed as he rolled the dice.

"Five," he said, counting out spaces on the game board with his thimble. "Reading Railroad. . . . Yes! I'll buy it!"

He quickly shelled out the money to the Scout who was acting as game banker.

In other corners of the Scout room, other boys were also playing the popular board game. Cheers and jeers alternated with moans and groans as the games progressed.

After about twenty minutes of play, Scoutmaster Steve Marshall walked to the middle of the room and cleared his throat.

"I need everyone to listen for a minute," he said. "We're going to change a few rules before we continue. First of all, how many of you own railroads or utilities?"

He looked around as four or five Scouts raised their hands. He nodded.

"Okay," he said. "You boys need to sell those properties back to the bank. The bankers will give you $200 apiece for them. And from now on, the bank owns all railroads and utilities . . . no one can buy them, and rent to the bank is whatever you're normally required to pay."

He held up a restraining hand as shouts of protest filled the room.

"I'm sorry," he said, though he really didn't sound sorry at all. "But those are the rules. And"—he looked directly at a Scout who was particularly vocal—"I don't want to hear any more whining about it."

He waited until the moaning had died to a few murmurs before continuing.

"And here's another rule," he said. "No matter what it says on the card, rent on all personal properties is $200. And whenever you collect rent from another player, you must give half of it to the bank."

He paused as another chorus of protests filled the room. One Scout had even leaped to his feet.

"Does that include Boardwalk and Park Place?" he asked. "I've got hotels on them!"

Marshall nodded. "It includes everything. Now, I'll give you another fifteen or twenty minutes to play."

The boys returned to their games, but with considerably less enthusiasm than before. They played mechanically until Marshall finally directed them to stop. Then, after the games had been put away, the Scoutmaster began a discussion.

"How many of you enjoyed my new rules tonight?" he asked.

No one responded.

Marshall smiled. "I didn't think you would. But in a very basic way, that's the way life would be if you lived in some other countries. The state often owns all of the utilities and takes a good share of whatever profits you earn in business. It controls prices. It reduces your control over your own property."

Though the boys weren't initially excited by the prospect of a lecture, they were all listening. Marshall had captured their attention and piqued their interest. More important, he had discovered a way to help them understand the points he was making.

Marshall wasn't trying to impugn foreign governments that night. He wasn't promoting democracy. Instead, he was helping his troop to understand some of the differences between constitutional and non-constitutional forms of government so they could pass off Requirement Number Five of the Citizenship in the World Merit Badge.

The Boy Scout merit badge program was designed to lead boys through a series of learning experiences that promote citizenship, character, and personal fitness. It encourages them to sharpen their skills in things they like to do, and it challenges them to expand their horizons by exploring new activities. It gives Scouts opportunities to measure their accomplishments and to be rewarded for their efforts.

And because they are required for advancement, merit badges are an essential part of every boy's progress in Scouting.

Unfortunately, merit badge work can often become dull and tedious. Worse than that, because some badges require reports, research, and other sorts of paper work, working on them often isn't much different from being in school. So when you can find ways to inject a little life into merit badge work, you'll not only be making Scouting more fun, but you'll be making your own troop meetings more exciting too. And you'll be doing a great service to your boys.

Let's look at a few ways to do that.

## ELIMINATE THE CLASSROOM ATMOSPHERE

During the fall and winter months, teenage boys spend about six hours a day—five days a week—in school. And after they get home, they might have another hour or two of homework. So by the time they get to a troop meeting, sitting quietly in a chair and listening to a lecture will seem about as appealing as a trip to a drill-happy dentist.

The boys want action. They want fun! They want excitement.

So if you want to enhance your merit badge program, your first challenge is to put away the chairs and the chalkboard and put as much life and energy into your lessons as possible. You need to convince the boys that they're not in school.

When Scoutmaster Allen Hillman's troop was earning the Backpacking Merit Badge, he wanted to emphasize the importance of loading backpacks in a neat and orderly manner. And he wanted his Scouts to understand the importance of packing certain items such as first-aid kits, ponchos, matches, and water bottles where they could be retrieved in a hurry.

He knew that he could have explained all of this in troop meeting. But he wanted a more effective way to drive the point home.

So Hillman had the boys load their packs—tents, sleeping bags, and all—and took them on a hike through the neighborhood. After ten or fifteen minutes, he called for a short break.

"I think I'm getting a blister," he said. "I'll give a bag of raisins to the first Scout to give me a bandage."

Gear flew as Scouts dug into their packs. Then, a minute or so later—after he'd received a bandage and given away a bag of raisins—he said: "You never know when you're going to get a blister or some other injury while you're out hiking. So it's a good idea to keep your first-aid supplies where you can get them without a lot of fuss."

Another block or two down the road, he stopped again, saying, "I've got a bag of raisins for the first Scout to hand me his poncho."

The next instant everyone was again digging frantically through their packs. After Hillman had rewarded the winning Scout, he said, "You know, if it suddenly started raining in the middle of hike, you wouldn't want to waste a lot of time looking for your rain gear. So it's a good idea to keep it close, too. Now, what other items do you think you ought to keep handy?"

"Matches!" someone said.

Hillman nodded. "Matches, good," he said. "I've got a bag of raisins for the first Scout to hand me his matches."

Hillman didn't teach the boys anything that he couldn't have taught them back in the Scout room. But because he conducted his lesson out on the road, he made it more compelling and meaningful. He brought the concept to life.

But Hillman wasn't finished. When the boys reached the halfway point, he told everyone to stop and remove their packs.

"Who's tired?" he asked.

Several hands went up.

"Did you know that the way you pack your gear can actually make it easier to carry? Did you know there are tricks for making your pack feel lighter?" He looked at each of the boys. "Would you like me to show you?"

Did they ever!

Hillman then demonstrated how to raise a backpack's center of gravity by packing tents and other heavy gear on top. He showed the boys how to place hard items toward the outside of the bag where they wouldn't dig into the hiker's back, as well as other important tips. The boys spent several minutes repacking their gear before hiking back to the church, many of them exclaiming that their packs *did* feel better! And that they were easier to carry!

Again, Hillman didn't do anything that he couldn't have done back in the Scout room. But by waiting until the boys saw a need for his lesson, he made his instructions more effective.

There are many lessons that you can teach effectively on the chalkboard back in the Scout room. And there are probably some that you wouldn't want to teach any other way. But any time you can eliminate a school-like atmosphere, you'll not only be adding variety to your Scouts' experience, but you'll be making your lessons more interesting too.

## GO BEYOND THE REQUIREMENTS

When a Scout is being tested by a qualified merit badge

counselor, he must be tested exactly as the requirements specify. He cannot be asked to do any more or any less than required by the official merit badge pamphlet.

But while you're *teaching* a particular skill or concept— while you're *preparing* your Scouts to pass off the requirements—you are free to embellish all you want.

When my troop went to Thunder Ridge Boy Scout Camp, most of the boys signed up for rifle shooting, which turned out to be one of the most interesting classes of the week. The reason was that the instructor knew his subject so well that he went far beyond the nuts and bolts of the merit badge, keeping the boys spellbound with facts and anecdotes that kept the boys glued to their seats. At the end of each session, he practically had to shoo all the boys away to their next classes.

Richard Marks, a Scoutmaster I met at summer camp, once helped his troop earn the Swimming Merit Badge at a neighborhood pool. One requirement called for each Scout to swim fifty yards using inflated clothing for support. But Marks went a step further and organized a game of water polo with each boy inflating his pants and using them to float on as they played.

The activity not only built the boys' confidence in this life-saving technique, but it gave them considerable practice at it. Besides that, the boys had a lot of fun.

And when his troop was earning Lifesaving, Marks noticed that Scouts were required to demonstrate their ability to tow a tired swimmer.

"I saw that and *knew* we had to make a game of it," he said. "So we put together an obstacle course in the swimming pool and ran relays."

Besides turning lifesaving into an exciting adventure,

Marks taught his boys skills in a way they weren't likely to forget.

Merit badge requirements are designed so that Scouts can demonstrate the proficiency of their skills. But they are not comprehensive. By teaching beyond the requirements, you can get beyond the nitty-gritty nuts and bolts of the coursework and explore the excitement. You can help your Scouts to become even more proficient than the badge requires.

And you can make it a lot of fun in the process.

## TEACH YOUR SCOUTS THE IMPORTANCE OF THE SKILLS THEY'RE LEARNING

Most Scouts have little interest in skills that they see no reason for. But if they truly believe that a certain skill might one day come in handy, they'll be more eager to become even better at it.

To earn the Lifesaving Merit Badge, Scouts are required to show that they can remove their street clothes on shore in less than twenty seconds. And though most Scouts wear their swimming suits beneath their clothes as they do this, many of them nevertheless feel silly doing it.

"The boys think it's a silly requirement," said Ryan Dixon, a long-time aquatics director. "And a lot of kids don't think it's important. The problem is that when someone's really in trouble, many people jump into the water fully clothed when they go to help. They don't understand how dangerous that can be."

So to drive the point home, Dixon has his lifesaving classes swim relays fully clothed. "We swim laps, retrieve objects from underwater, and have races wearing normal street clothes," he said. "Then we put on our swimming suits and do it all again. The boys learn firsthand how difficult—

and dangerous—it is to attempt a rescue fully clothed."

When I was the program director at Camp Maple Dell, we were required to conduct an emergency fire drill every week. That always annoyed me because the drills cut into our time and interrupted the flow of our camp program.

But one week, just before dinner, we spotted black smoke billowing above the trees up the canyon. There was a fire, and it was headed our way.

It turned out the fire wasn't serious, and it wasn't long before the Forest Service had it under control. But in those first, anxious moments, I was overwhelmed with gratitude that we had an evacuation plan and that we had practiced it. And I never again complained or hesitated when it came time to schedule a drill.

Your boys will be the same way. When they know *why* certain things have to be done, when they know *why* certain skills and tasks are required, they'll be more patient about doing them.

A Scoutmaster named Derek Wiscombe told me how an unusually strong windstorm once wreaked havoc in his neighborhood. It knocked down trees and power lines and caused thousands of dollars of damage to people's homes. Power was expected to be off for at least one day, and possibly two or three more.

"People were panicking," Wiscombe told me, "because many of them simply weren't prepared. So we began working on Emergency Preparedness that very week, beginning with the requirement to create personal emergency packs. Many of the boys had been without power that week— some of them for a whole day or two—and they understood. They knew why it was important and they were even more anxious than usual to participate."

### PROVIDE INSTANT RECOGNITION

When a boy has successfully completed all of the requirements for a merit badge, he should receive it at the very next meeting. You can present it in a small ceremony at the beginning or close of the meeting, but be sure to do it. This is the method described in the Scoutmaster's Handbook, and it is more effective than making a boy wait several weeks until the next court of honor.

Besides that—since he may be the only Scout receiving a badge that particular night—it may give him the chance to stand in the spotlight all by himself for a few moments. That alone is often motivation enough to have him out working hard on the next one.

Then, at the next court of honor, you can recognize him again by mentioning all of the badges he has earned since the last ceremony.

Advancement is one of the key methods of achieving citizenship, character, and personal fitness in the Boy Scout program. And because merit badges are such a crucial part of that, they are vital to your boys' progress within the Boy Scout program.

So make merit badges exciting to work on. Make them fun to earn. And your boys will not only be having fun in Scouting, but you'll be having the time of your life too.

## HOW TO GET STARTED!

 **Consider the next skill you're planning to teach.** To break the routine, see if there isn't some way to teach your lesson outside, in a park, or in the foothills.

**To make your lessons more effective,** first find some way to expose your Scouts to the problem. Let them carry their packs for a mile or two before offering to show them a more efficient way to pack their gear. Let them try to build a fire with damp wood or thick sticks before introducing the idea of kindling.

 **The next time you're preparing** to teach a merit badge and are looking over the requirements, see if there isn't one or two that you could turn into a game or contest. Do the boys need to make something? Have a contest! Do they need to demonstrate a skill? Have a race! (As you do this, be mindful of those boys who may not often win. Look for ways that they can shine and excel too!)

 **Rather than teach everything yourself,** see if there are some skills the boys could teach one another. Is anyone particularly good at knots? Let him teach his friends! Have a good swimmer in the troop? Let him share his secrets!

 **Provide instant recognition.** When a boy earns a merit badge, present it to him at the very next meeting. Remember that you can still recognize him at the next court of honor, but don't make him wait.

# 5

# CAN ANYONE TIE A
# TIMBER HITCH?

## PUTTING THE FUN IN SCOUTCRAFT

Fourteen-year-old Javin Carter burst into the Scout room with a look of horror on his face.

"Quick!" he shouted. "Sam's burned himself in the kitchen! You've got to come quick!"

In an instant, the entire troop was thundering toward the kitchen. Sam, one of the troop's patrol leaders, was lying on the floor writhing in pain.

"Help me!" he screamed. "Please help me! It hurts!"

The Scouts gasped as Sam squirmed on the floor. The boy's shirt had been badly scorched and the flesh was peeling away from third-degree burns on his arm.

A Scout named Aaron was the first to respond.

"Jordan!" he yelled to a nearby Scout as he knelt beside

his injured friend. "We need bandages! Lots of them!"

"And a sheet," a boy named Steve yelled, kneeling opposite Aaron. "Hurry!"

Robert Janke, the troop Scoutmaster, stood out of the way as the boys treated the injured Scout. After all, as terrible as Sam looked, he wasn't really hurt. Before the meeting, Janke had covered the boy's arm with a mixture of petroleum jelly and red food dye, dabbing in a few strips of toilet paper to simulate peeling flesh and sprinkling on ground-up charcoal to create the appearance of charred skin.

The resulting "burn" looked horrifyingly real.

More than that, it brought life to the troop's first-aid practice.

By the time most boys have been Scouts for a couple of years, they've tied hundreds of knots, treated dozens of imaginary wounds, and built countless fires. And while these are important skills that need to be reviewed and practiced often, they sometimes become so repetitious and ordinary that many boys begin losing interest in them.

Worse than that, many boys are never actually taught the importance of Scoutcraft. They never learn the practical value of the skills they spend so much time learning and passing off. They learn how to tie the timber hitch, for instance, but they never learn why they'd ever need to. (Think quick . . . when *do* you need a timber hitch? When do you use a sheet bend? Don't know? If your Scouts don't know, there's no way they can ever possibly put their skills to use.)

The challenge, then, is to teach Scoutcraft in a way that makes it fun and exciting, making certain the boys know how to apply the skills once they've mastered them.

I used to work at Boy Scout Camp Maple Dell with an eighteen-year-old boy named Tucker. He was the camp nature director and one of the most creative Scouters I've ever known. He could take the most ordinary lesson and turn it into a remarkable adventure. Scouts who had already earned Nature and Environmental Science often signed up for those classes anyway because Tucker made them so much fun.

Each Friday afternoon, for instance, Maple Dell conducted camp-wide Scoutcraft competitions, and one week Tucker was assigned the knot-tying relays.

He was aghast.

"Knot tying?" he protested. "Why do we have to have knot tying?"

Jack Brown, the camp program director, spread his hands. "We always have knot tying."

"That's my point," Tucker said. "Scouts tie knots everywhere they go. They tie them in troop meetings, they tie them for merit badges, and they tie them on campouts. By the time they come to Scout camp they're sick of them!"

Jack just shrugged. "Well, then this ought to be a good chance to find a way to make them fun."

Tucker opened his mouth to protest further, then stopped. And I knew him well enough to know what he was thinking—he *could* find a way to make them fun.

To make the effect as dramatic as possible, Tucker refused to tell anyone what he had in mind, but he made certain everyone knew it was going to be spectacular . . . and that this week, knot tying would be conducted at the swimming pool!

I was so curious that wild horses couldn't have kept me away from the swimming pool that Friday afternoon. And Tucker didn't disappoint me.

Tucker had the boys tying knots, all right. But he had the Scouts tying them around poles, tubes, and buoys floating in the middle of the pool. He had taken a zany idea, thrown in a dash of crazy, stirred in a little goofiness, and then cranked up the ridiculous. The result was a relay that had boys clamoring for more, and when the Scouts listed their favorite activities of the week, most of them ranked knot tying—knot tying!—right up there with canoe swamping.

If you're going to spend much time as a Scoutmaster, then Scoutcraft is certain to be an important part of your program. And if you really want the boys to listen—if you really want them to learn important Scout skills—you'll need to capture their interest and hold their attention.

Here are a couple of ideas:

### TEACH SKILLS IN WAYS THE BOYS HAVE NEVER SEEN BEFORE

Every boy has tied knots, for instance, so find ways for them to have fun while they're doing it. Every boy has built fires, so create new pyrotechnic challenges for them to conquer.

Ben Jackson, a Scoutmaster I met at Maple Dell, shared with me a method for combining Scoutcraft skills with bad-weather training. "We take the troop down to the park and have the boys pitch tents and build fires," he told me. "But we spray them with garden hoses while they do it."

Jackson said that any Scout who can start a fire in those conditions certainly has the skill to build one during a mountain rainstorm. "And how else are they going to learn to pitch a tent in the rain and keep all of their gear dry while they do it?" he asked. "Besides, you've never seen boys have more fun. . . . We invite their parents come out to watch, and before it's all over we generally end up having a spectacular water fight."

Another Scoutmaster, looking for ways to liven up ordinary compass work, took his troop out at night. A few nights earlier, his patrol leaders hiked into the local foothills and secured bits of reflective tape to branches, rocks, and brush, creating a fun, challenging course. Then the Scouts, using compasses and flashlights, raced to find their way from one marker to the next, knowing when they spotted the bits of reflecting tape that they'd identified the correct course.

Tucker, the boy I introduced earlier in this chapter, used to take Scouts on a unique nature hike. Most boys, he knew, had been on ordinary, run-of-the-mill nature hikes before, so he began by promising that this one would be different. "We're not going to identify plants and animals like you usually do on nature hikes," he said. "Instead, we're going to use our senses. We're going to go out and taste things. . . . We're going to go out and smell things, hear things, see things, and touch things."

Just that fast, Tucker had the undivided attention of every Scout in the class. And he lived up to his promise. As the boys followed him through the forest, they tasted wild strawberries, smelled the cinnamon-scented bark of Ponderosa Pines, listened to the wind in the canyon, examined and discussed the red rocks of the cliffs, and felt the sharp cutting edges of flint and obsidian pieces.

It was unlike any nature hike the boys had ever experienced.

If you want to bring out the true fun of Scoutcraft, get away from traditional activities. Find ways to make them different.

## FIND WAYS TO MAKE SCOUTCRAFT SKILLS COME TO LIFE

Robert Janke, the Scoutmaster I introduced at the beginning of this chapter, had a knack for bringing Scoutcraft skills to life. Rather than simply reviewing the same, tiring first-aid tips that his Scouts had heard dozens of times before, he livened up the subject by creating realistic wounds and injuries for the boys to treat. In addition to burns, he created cuts, bruises, punctures, and all sorts of other gruesome and gory injuries.

"Our first-aid relay is so much fun that the boys' parents and bishopric often show up to watch," he said.

Janke starts by dressing up a victim for each patrol. These "victims" are given burns, broken arms, nails impaled in their hands, and sometimes even eyeballs that dangle from their faces. (Janke tells the boys, "These kids have really had a bad day!")

When the relay begins, each Scout treats and dresses one injury, then races back to the patrol, tagging the next Scout, who then races into action. Afterward, all the dressings are evaluated and critiqued.

"Most times we don't have to say a whole lot," Janke said. "The boys can usually tell us what they've done right or wrong, and they often ask for a chance to correct their mistakes." Janke likes to go a step further by allowing his Scouts to become part of the creative process, inviting patrols to create their own unusual first-aid cases for the others to deal with. The boys are not only able to create their own gruesome injuries, but they evaluate the Scouts who attempt to assess and treat them.

"By making up their own injuries and watching others treat them, the boys really learn a lot of first aid," he told me. "When someone has a cut finger, a nosebleed, or a broken bone, it's usually not too tough to figure out what's wrong. But learning to identify heat stroke or hypothermia is a little more tricky. Besides, the boys have a great time doing it. Our first-aid month is always one of the highlights of the year."

Janke said that another benefit is that Scouts accustomed

to hands-on training are usually more likely to take action when disaster strikes for real.

"It can be frightening to jump in and act when someone's hurt," said. "But when Scouts are already used to doing the work, when they've already developed the confidence of knowing what to do, it becomes like 'muscle memory.' They jump right in and go to work."

Another Scoutmaster brought compass skills to life by creating what he called "madman scenarios." Taking his Scouts to a nearby park, he said, "You've just been told that a crazy man has set a bomb to blow up in twenty minutes. You've found his secret map, and you have to follow it to find the bomb before it goes off."

And with that, the boys used their compasses to follow a course around the park, knowing they had only minutes to find the hidden "bomb." (Using a cooking timer that actually buzzed if not found and disarmed in time added an extra element of excitement to the game.)

Making a Scoutcraft skill come to life not only takes it out of the ordinary, but makes it more fun and exciting. It allows boys to use their imagination. And it gives the Scouts practice with skills that they often don't realize they're learning.

## GIVE THE SCOUTS INCENTIVES FOR LEARNING THE SKILLS YOU'RE TEACHING

If you want to teach fire-building, give your boys a reason for building a fire. (Like a pot of water that needs to be boiled.) If you want to teach them knots and lashings, be sure to have the materials for building a bridge or tower outside.

I know one troop that spent time learning to make and splice ropes. Then, every boy was asked to make a six-foot rope, tying an eye-splice in one end and an end-splice in the other. The ropes were then joined together and used for tugs-o-war, commando games, and other activities. The boys all knew that if any of the ropes broke, their patrol would lose the contest, so everyone was careful to do their best work.

Another troop created fun incentives by establishing records. They had troop records for tying the one-handed bowline, building bow drill fires, and reciting the alphabet in Morse Code. And it was a great source of motivation. A Scout named Tom once started a flint-and-steel fire in two minutes and thirty-seven seconds. Then, after another Scout beat his record by eighteen seconds, Tom worked for days practicing and perfecting his technique. Finally, during troop meeting, he took one of the assistant Scoutmasters into the parking lot and started a fire in a minute twenty seconds.

Not only do such records inspire fun and competition, but they go a long way toward building self-esteem within the boys who set them. More than that, any boy who learns a skill well enough to set a record has truly come close to mastering that skill. (Imagine a troop in which every Scout was best, fastest, or greatest at something!)

## INTRODUCE THE ELEMENT OF CHALLENGE

When you practice fire-building, try using damp wood. When you tie knots, blindfold everyone. When you practice compass skills, have the boys follow a compass course at night. When you do first aid, don't give the boys splints or bandages to work with . . . see how creative and innovative they can be treating wounds with only the materials they happen to find laying around.

One week when my friend Tucker couldn't use the camp swimming pool for his knot relays, he divided Scouts into pairs, gave each one a six-foot length of rope, and directed them to a line of stakes in the ground. Each stake had a three-foot circle drawn around it.

"You have to tie a clove hitch around your stake," he explained. "And you can't cross the circle to do it."

Tucker's activity had the boys tying knots, all right. But his unusual stipulations turned ordinary knots into a stimulating challenge.

Another idea is to combine different, unrelated skills. Remember knots and swimming? Well, how about combining compass work with, say, boating? (Can you imagine how fun it would be to run an orienteering course in a canoe?) Or how about combining first aid with pioneering? Or camping and citizenship?

This is another opportunity to let the Scouts get involved in the creative process. Take several slips of paper and on each one list some skill such as knots and lashings, cooking, first aid, or nature study. On several others list activities such as aquatics, relay races, and archery. Place the first slips in one bowl, and the second slips in another. Then invite someone to draw a slip of paper from each bowl and challenge the Scouts to invent an activity that combines the two skills. You'll be surprised at the wild, exotic ideas a group of motivated boys can come up with. More than that, you'll be surprised at the fun and excitement they'll have doing it.

## GIVE YOUR SCOUTS OPPORTUNITIES TO TEACH WHAT THEY'VE LEARNED

After all, no one knows a skill as well as someone who can teach it. A few weeks after setting the troop record for building a flint-and-steel fire, Tom was invited to demonstrate his skill to younger Scouts who hadn't yet learned it. Other boys, adept at fire-building, archery, or cooking, had chances to teach their skills to younger Scouts too.

It's one thing to learn a new skill and quite another to actually pass it off to an adult leader. But imagine the proficiency boys develop by passing on their newfound skills to younger, inexperienced boys.

Scoutcraft skills are such a routine part of Scouting that they often become mundane and tedious. But with a dash of imagination and a spark of creativity, they can energize your Scouting program. They can literally breathe new life into your next troop meeting or campout. So look for ways to bring otherwise "ordinary" skills to life. Let the boys see what fun Scouting can be!

## HOW TO GET STARTED!

 **Think of the next Scoutcraft** skill you have listed on your calendar. Now, let your imagination go wild. Start thinking "outside the box." What about daytime astronomy, for instance? (Try having the boys place rocks or marbles in the shape of constellations.) See if you can't come up with ways to bring that skill to life. Figure out how to teach it in a new and creative way.

 **Try combining two skills into one.** Like orienteering and skiing. Or nature study and first aid. Or what about emergency preparedness and cooking? (Let the boys experience what it would be like to prepare a meal with only the emergency supplies they might have after an earthquake, flood, or hurricane.)

**Let your boys help to devise new activities.** Challenge them to come up with a new, exciting way to learn citizenship. Let them find a creative method for practicing back-country cooking.

 **Whatever skill you teach,** be sure to show the boys *why* it's important that they learn it. Show them why they need to know the timber hitch and why they should be able to read a map. Give them practical examples and real-life applications to practice on.

# 6

## MOOSECAPADES AND
# PESKY MOSQUITOES

### PUTTING THE FUN IN PATROLS

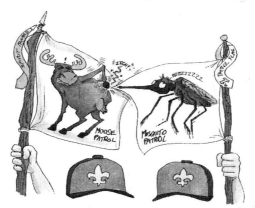

**F**rogs, report!"

Senior Patrol Leader Scott Brady was holding a clipboard as he stood in front of the Frog Patrol.

No one answered.

Scott looked up in surprise. "Frogs?"

Brian Gardner, a Star Scout who was the Frogs' patrol leader, pursed his lips nonchalantly. He waited another moment, then looked up innocently. "Oh . . . are you talking to us?"

"Yes!"

"We're not the Frog Patrol . . ."

Scott opened his mouth to say something, then looked over at Scoutmaster Harris. The Scoutmaster shrugged patiently and gestured for Scott to play along.

"Okay, then . . . who are you?"

Brian snapped to attention. "We're the Moose Patrol!"

"Okay, then . . . Moose, report!"

Brian turned and led the Moose in their patrol song:

Oh . . . the . . . cannibal moose
With the big caboose
Went out on the lake one day . . .

I grinned as I watched what later came to be known as the "Moosecapades." For me, this was always one of the most entertaining parts of our weekly troop meeting. After our opening activity, Scott lined the troop's patrols up for uniform inspection and spirit competition. He inspected each patrol for attendance and uniforming and then allowed the boys to perform their patrol song or yell.

Scott awarded points for each portion of the inspection and gave the winning patrol the troop spirit stick for the week. (This was nothing more than an old walking stick decorated with feathers and strips of leather, but winning it was considered a great accomplishment.) The competition was so keen that the rival patrols began wearing immaculate uniforms, and they were constantly inventing new songs and yells, as well as devising clever antics in order to win.

Patrol competition was never dull!

At any rate, the next week Scott lined the patrols up as usual.

"Moose . . . report!"

There was no response.

Brian rocked quietly on his heels.

"Moose?"

Brian looked up absently. "Oh . . . are you talking to us? We're not the Moose."

"You were the Moose last week!"

Brian looked shocked. "We were never!" He beamed proudly. "We're the Grizzlies!"

And with that, he led the patrol in its new song. It was two verses long this time. The first verse lauded the Grizzlies, and the second verse was the same Moose stanza as the week before.

The next week was pretty much the same, except that the Frogs/Moose/Grizzlies claimed they were now the King Cobras. And their patrol song was three verses long. It reached the point that during spirit competition, Scott simply asked, "Well, who are you this week?"

Because I was the assistant Scoutmaster assigned to advise them, I told Brian that it was fun to see them being so creative but suggested that they choose a single patrol mascot and stick with it.

"But we have!" Brian insisted.

"What is it?"

"It's a secret!"

I tried pressing him, but neither Brian nor anyone else in the patrol would talk. Apparently they had selected a secret mascot, and they weren't about to tell anyone what it was.

Not, that is, until the next court of honor. By then, they were the Frogs/Moose/Grizzlies/King Cobras/Marines/Muskrats/High Council/Sharpshooters/Tigers/Huskies, and their song was an excruciating nine verses long. It turned out that their secret mascot was the Chameleon, which was why they kept changing.

Hoo, boy.

Robert Baden-Powell, the founder of Scouting, once

said that the patrol method was not a way to run a Boy Scout troop. He said it was the *only* way. And I've never seen anything that could spark enthusiasm in a group of Scouts as much as a patrol that was fun to belong to. For many Scouts, much of that fun begins with zany patrol songs and yells.

Scoutmaster Bob Dixon once told me about a group of Scouts who called themselves the Mosquitoes. An important Mosquito tradition dictated that they perform their patrol yell any time they heard their patrol name. At the top of their lungs they'd yell, "Mosquitoes?"

And then—looking frantically in all directions as if searching for a pesky skeeter—they'd make a loud buzzing sound that increased in pitch and urgency over several seconds until they finally clapped their hands together— "Smack!"—as if dispatching the insect.

This, of course, was extremely annoying to everyone except the Mosquitoes. So to avoid unnecessary delays, the senior patrol leader had to conduct troop business while trying to avoid saying the word "Mosquitoes."

"Okay," he might say, "the Eagles are in charge of flag ceremony next week and the other patrol will set up the Scout room."

The Mosquitoes would eagerly lean forward in their chairs, asking in unison, "Who?"

"You know," the senior patrol leader would say with a sigh, "you guys."

"Who?"

The SPL would shift uncomfortably. "You guys . . . the Bug Scouts . . ."

The Mosquitoes pressed him relentlessly. "Who?"

Eventually the senior patrol leader had to give in. "Oh, all right . . . I'll say it! Mosquitoes!"

"MOSQUITOES? BzzzzzzzzzzzSMACK!"

When you can take a patrol and fill it with pride, competition, and spirit, half your job as Scoutmaster will be over. You won't have to coax boys into coming to meetings because they'll want to be there. You won't have to remind them to wear their uniforms—patrol pride and positive peer pressure will take care of that. And you won't have to hound them into earning merit badges. As long as Scouts in one patrol are progressing through the ranks, boys in the other will be hustling to keep up. Your troop will have such momentum that any boy within Doppler-radar range will be sucked in by the whirlwind and hurled toward the rank of Eagle.

In our troop, patrol spirit did more than inspire zany songs and yells. Each week, the patrols took turns conducting an opening flag ceremony. For a while, this meant little more than marching in with a flag, standing halfheartedly, and mumbling the Scout Oath. But one night, the Eagles decided to step outside the box, posting several historical flags around the Scout room and delivering a short presentation on flag etiquette.

Afterward, the Scoutmaster praised the Eagles for their thoughtfulness and patriotism.

I saw Brian's eyes narrow as he listened, and I could almost see the wheels spinning in his head. Few boys enjoyed patrol competition more than Brian, and now that his rivals had raised the bar, I knew he'd be planning some way to spice-up his own patrol's flag ceremony. And he didn't let me down. The next week, the Frogs told the story of Francis Scott Key and "The Star Spangled Banner." The patrol had a tape of cannons and rifle fire playing in the background, and I felt chills up and down my back as they conducted their ceremony.

The flag ceremony, traditionally a dull, routine part of troop meeting, had suddenly become one of the highlights of the evening.

Another troop I know used patrol competition to enhance week-long summer camp. As soon as each patrol was given a spot to camp—and told that awards would be given for the best campsite—the competition was on. When one patrol constructed a fence around its campsite, another responded by building a gate out of pioneering poles, complete with a rotating turnstile. When one patrol built a levitating flagpole (trust me . . . Google it), the other countered with a twenty-foot tower . . . and then spent the night sleeping on it.

But it didn't stop there. The rival patrols competed for the honor of having the Scoutmaster or favorite camp staff members to dinner, they hustled to earn merit badges, and they were excited to complete service projects. Simple patrol competition had taken a fun camping adventure, pumped it full of energy and excitement, and transformed it into a fantastic Scouting experience.

Your troop can experience the same miracle.

So if you really want a showcase troop, if you really want a troop that's full of life and energy and driven by the power of its own momentum, develop patrol spirit. Encourage creativity. Let the boys create fun patrol mascots and help them to come up with rousing cheers, yells, and songs. Let them compete with one another.

And don't be afraid to do the same thing on a troop basis too. There's nothing as impressive at camps or exhibitions as a sharp-looking troop of Scouts singing at the top of its collective lungs.

How do you get the boys started?

Easy! Just take a deep breath, gird up your loins, and do it!

Several years ago, I had the opportunity of teaching the Field Sports section of the National Camping School. The members of my section were mostly older men—all of them grizzled outdoorsmen and former military types—training to run the rifle and archery ranges at various Boy Scout camps.

Patrol songs?

Yells?

They weren't the least bit interested.

"That's cute," one of the men growled when the camp staff proudly belted out their zany staff song, complete with entertaining steps and gestures. "Go sing it somewhere else."

"Yeah, I know what you're thinking," I told the guys later at our first patrol meeting. "You're all embarrassed to sing and be silly in front of everyone else."

There was a round of nods and a few grumbles of, "You're darn right."

"But," I continued, "everyone else will be doing it. No one's going to think you're silly. And if you really get into the spirit of this—if you'll just break the ice and give it a try—I promise you that this week will be a thousand percent more fun for all of you."

The men weren't excited, but they were good sports. They put their heads together and decided to call themselves the Wildebeests. (Their patrol motto was, "No Gnus is Good Gnus.") They sewed small leather "horns" to their hats and attached curly leather strips that resembled wildebeest tails to their shirt pockets. Then at flag ceremonies and other official gatherings—whenever another camp member did something praiseworthy—they'd award a similar tail to the man and induct him as an honorary member of the patrol.

On top of that, they came up with such a unique, catchy

patrol song that the members of other patrols often whistled and even sang it as the week progressed.

But what really excited me about the Wildebeests was the unity they developed as a patrol. At meal times, as everyone gathered in the dining hall, one member would softly begin singing their patrol song. Another Wildebeest would hear it and join in. Heads would rise above the crowd as other patrol members joined in, looking eagerly around for their "pards." They'd quickly gather together, still singing, and finish off their song at the tops of their lungs. (They concluded every performance by snapping to attention and saying in unison, "And that's the gnus . . . now for the weather and sports.")

Men who had resisted the idea of singing and engaging in other silly patrol shenanigans were suddenly the envy of the camp. They were the top patrol, and though they were initially reluctant to even participate, they were suddenly the patrol that everyone else looked to for ideas and motivation.

So how does that apply to you?

Well, if a bunch of grumpy old men can learn to enjoy patrol spirit, your energy-filled teenagers can too. Yes, some of them might seem reluctant at first, but don't give up. Once the ice is broken, the hard part's over.

And what if you don't have all that many boys?

Do it anyway! Even if you only have one patrol, the boys can still make up songs, yells, and flags. At Scout camp one year, one troop showed up—with just one boy. His father was the Scoutmaster, and the two of them comprised the entire troop. But that didn't slow them down one bit. At morning flag ceremony they sang and competed with Super Troops made up of dozens of Scouts. Rival troops were as anxious to see them perform as the largest, goofiest, most flamboyant groups.

The father and son had taken what everyone believed was a liability and made it work for them.

As Lord Baden-Powell said, the patrol method is not a way to run a Boy Scout troop—it's the only way. So get started! Let the magic of patrols energize your troop, making Scouting even more exciting, even more compelling, and even more fun!

## HOW TO GET STARTED!

 **Unless you have a troop** with only two or three boys, be certain to use the patrol method. Be sure to divide them evenly so that each patrol is equally strong in regards to talent, creativity, and personality.

 **Lead by example!** Invent a Scoutmaster song or yell and challenge the boys to be more zany—or to perform more enthusiastically—than you and your assistants. (Invite the ward bishop to judge the contest.)

 **Encourage creativity.** Encourage the Scouts to choose creative, unusual mascots that will develop pride and loyalty. Allow the boys to make flags and create songs and yells.

 **Once you've established patrols,** be sure to use them. Assign duties such as opening activities and flag ceremonies on a patrol basis, and on campouts encourage patrol spirit by having patrols camp and cook together.

# 7

# CHASING THE ELUSIVE
# SASQUATCH

## PUTTING THE FUN IN NIGHT ACTIVITIES

Over to the left just a little bit . . . no, the other way . . . okay, there! Now, hold it!"

Jeff Barton was looking over the top of his compass as his partner, Tyler Payne, marked a spot in the trees thirty feet away. Jeff took a moment to make certain his compass bearing was exactly right, then pointed his flashlight at Tyler.

"Okay . . . that's the way: right past Tyler toward that tall tree over there. The card says we have to go forty-five yards."

The next instant the entire patrol was busy pacing off steps through the forest. They had only gone a short distance before someone let out a shout.

"There it is! I see it!"

Forgetting about pacing, the boys dashed for a piece of reflective tape sparkling in the beam of their flashlights. Jeff quickly pulled out his instruction card.

"All right . . . the next one is 155 degrees, sixty yards." He spun the dial of his compass, waited for the needle to settle, then pointed off into the forest. "Okay . . . it's over that way, toward that weird-looking tree."

The patrol was following a compass course just like many others they'd followed as Boy Scouts. The only difference was that this time they were doing it in the middle of the night.

Night is often a time of little excitement for Scout troops. At summer camp, and on weekend campouts, dinner is prepared and eaten, the dishes washed and put away, and after standing around the campfire for a few minutes or playing a game of Capture the Flag, everyone begins getting ready for bed. (Either that, or they begin preparing for a night of mischief.)

But nighttime offers many of Scouting's most exciting challenges. It not only provides unique opportunities to work on merit badges, but it adds challenges and adventures that are hard to duplicate in the light of day.

The Sasquatch Challenge that had Jeff and Tyler and their patrol up until all hours was part of a night activity program at Camp Maple Dell. Dashing through the trees in an attempt to beat the camp record of fifty-two minutes, the boys honed their compass skills, learned to judge distances, and developed teamwork. On top of all that, they had a blast!

That particular course was set up in the forest, of course, but it didn't have to be. It just as easily could have been set up in a city park or around the neighborhood.

When I directed the Beaver High Adventure Base in southern Utah, my aquatics director conducted evening activities that were almost as popular as the swimming, canoeing, and sailing events he supervised during the day. He was an avid astronomer and often took Scouts out in rowboats to look at stars and constellations. He knew all of the major ones, and he could identify prominent stars such as Antares ("It's 400 times larger than our sun.") and Arcturus. ("It's a red star—which means it's a cool star—but it's hard to see the color without a telescope.") He could also point out any of the planets that happened to be wandering by that particular time of year.

"Look up at the Big Dipper," I once heard him tell a group of Scouts as he traced the constellation with the beam of his flashlight. "Do you see the stars that make up the handle? Well, this one closest to the bowl is 66 light years away. And that one at the far end of the handle is 210 light years away. Up there in the sky they look like they're pretty close together, don't they? But we're actually closer to that first star than it is to the other one."

(When I asked Travis how he knew all of this, he just shrugged. "I read about it in the Astronomy Merit Badge pamphlet," he said.)

After gazing up at the stars for half an hour or so, everyone rowed back to shore, where his staff had hot chocolate and Dutch-oven cobbler waiting.

A Scoutmaster named Steven Jeffs told me that he once conducted a similar activity with his troop.

"There are several meteor showers during the summer," he explained. "So when my troop was working on astronomy, we organized a meteor campout. We spent the night laying in our sleeping bags, talking, and looking up at the stars," he said "We happened to catch a good shower that night and saw one meteor right after the other."

Jeffs explained that on the right nights, observers can see anywhere from five to a hundred meteors an hour, and though the relative darkness of the mountains might be more conducive to astronomy, Scouts are also likely to see meteors while camping in the city park, behind the church building, or even in someone's backyard.

"Activities like that take very little effort," he said. "All you have to do is lie back in your sleeping bag and watch. It's great fun!"

Scoutmaster Bruce Richins dreamed up another creative nighttime activity. He took a topographic map of the area his troop was camping in, burned off the edges, and glued it to a piece of blue paper so that it looked like the map of an island.

"This is a treasure map," he told the boys. "We're down here on one end, and you've got to get to the other side to find the treasure. The only thing is that there are six landmarks you've got to find and stop at along the way. They're all marked on the map."

"What do we do at the landmarks?" someone asked.

"There'll be a white feather for you to pick up at each one," Richins said. "Along with some sort of prize. You need to bring me all the feathers so I know that you found them . . . and I think you'll know what to do with your prizes."

By the time the troop set off into the forest it was nearly ten o'clock. And because the course was a little more than two miles round trip, it was well past midnight by the time the boys finished.

But at every landmark, Richins not only had a feather waiting, but he also had a bag of candy, a pot of punch, or a bag of raisins to help keep the boys motivated.

"I set up night hikes like that about twice a year," he told me. "They're easy enough that the boys don't need extensive compass or map-reading skills to follow them, and sometimes I'll give the hike a spy theme or something. I always have the boys carry a cell phone, and sometimes, when they reach their landmarks, they'll have to call me to find out where I've hidden their prize."

Richins emphasized that the boys stick together as they hike (as well as having an assistant Scoutmaster tagging along) and that sometimes he has them collect samples of different trees or plants or even different kinds of bugs.

"It's a great adventure," he said. "And I've had many Scouts conquer fears of darkness and mountains by doing it. They get out there with their friends and have a good time, and they learn that there's nothing there that's going to hurt them."

Night adventures are only limited by your own imagination. But if you have a hard time being creative, just think up a couple of activities that are popular during the day and see if you can't do any of them at night. You may be surprised at what you come up with. How about an evening nature hike, for instance? Or flashlight fishing? Obstacle courses, relay races, and tracking games are all activities that you can enjoy at night. When I was a Scout, my troop once spent an entire night visiting local stores, warehouses, and all-night manufacturing plants, learning about occupations that involved night work, then returned to the church just in time for breakfast.

Years later, when I became an assistant Scoutmaster, my

troop spent a week at Thunder Ridge Scout Camp, where we were invited to a round of flashlight archery. The mere sound of the activity was intriguing enough that there wasn't any problem getting the boys excited. And it turned out to be the highlight of the week.

The archery director followed the same procedures as he did during the day, except that he had boys point dim flashlights toward the targets from the firing line. The flashlights weren't powerful enough to actually illuminate the targets, but small circles of reflective tape flickering in the darkness gave the boys an idea of where to aim.

We lost several arrows—I would have been surprised if we hadn't!—but the novelty of the experience was well worth the cost of replacing them. I never would have thought of trying archery at night, but it was properly supervised, safe, and, well, it was a blast! Not only that, but it gave the boys a chance to sharpen their skills and work on the Archery Merit Badge too.

There are thousands of other things you can try. I know one Scoutmaster who used the quiet evening hours to teach cooking skills. When the boys gathered around the campfire (like they always do at night), he'd pull out a Dutch oven and walk the boys through the process of making cobbler (he liked to pour a can of orange soda into the batter—"Don't stir it now! The soda makes orange stripes in the cobbler when it's finished!"—before placing it on the coals). The boys talked and told stories as the cobbler baked, then they had a delicious snack before going off to bed.

My favorite nighttime activities have always been campfires. For me, there's just nothing like capping a day of excitement and adventure with a little singing and storytelling around a cheery, crackling campfire. And when you want to talk seriously with the boys—about scriptures, missions, or other important topics—there's nothing that can beat the atmosphere created by a snapping campfire in the woods.

Scoutmasters often complain that they have a hard time remembering enough songs, skits, and stories to make their campfires meaningful. And I know the feeling! It's hard coming up with just the right song or story to fit the mood. So I always carry a small notebook with me. It's got every song, story, and joke I know, and any time I find myself needing an idea, it only takes a second to find just what I'm looking for.

But a word of caution here. If you're going to spend time around mountain campfires, you're certain to be asked for scary stories. Most boys love 'em, and many boys eagerly look forward to the organized ghost hikes offered at many Scout camps. Spooky stories and ghost hikes have their place, but remember that boys can often go too far with them. I used to work at a camp that offered a popular ghost hike. The only problem was that it was a little too scary. It got so out of hand that afterwards many boys refused to sleep in their own tents.

Moreover, there are some boys who may not want to participate in ghost hikes or other spooky activities but because of peer pressure will feel that they have no choice. Be mindful of these boys. Look for signs of reluctance and find ways to give those boys a way out.

If you don't like telling tales of sinister ghosts and hairy monsters—but the boys are insisting—you might do what Scoutmaster Roy Harris does. When the boys start bugging him for a scary story, he starts off with a tale that sounds like it's going to be harrowing. But then, as the mood and the story become darker and darker, he suddenly reaches a ridiculous, comical ending. And while the boys are laughing at the unexpected climax, he smoothly begins another story, subtly altering the mood of the campfire.

"Tell us something scary," I heard a boy ask him one night.

"Oh, let's not tell ghost stories tonight," he replied.

"Please," a second boy pleaded. "Tell us something really creepy!"

"Well," he said reluctantly, "I do remember something that happened to me once several years ago. . . . But I really don't like talking about it."

Five or six boys chimed in at once. "Tell us!"

"Well, I was out camping in the woods," he began in a hushed tone, still feigning reluctance. "It was a still, quiet night . . . but I suddenly heard a strange, rapping sound in the forest."

A young Scout looked up with wide eyes. "What was it?"

"I didn't know," he said in his most somber tone of voice. "But it went on and on until I knew I had to find out." He paused to heighten the suspense, then continued. "So I took my flashlight and carefully crept into the forest. All the time the strange, rapping sound was getting louder and louder. I'll tell you, I was really getting scared. And I almost turned back. But then . . . then I saw it!"

The boys couldn't stand the suspense. "What? What was it?"

Harris shrugged. "Wrapping paper."

When properly and safely conducted, night activities can add spice and variety to your program. Darkness not only adds the elements of mystery and challenge to your activities, but it provides interesting variety too.

So don't send the Scouts off to bed just because it gets a

little dark. Offer them a game of flashlight tag or a midnight compass course. Take them on a hike or conduct a campfire program.

Let them experience the fun of night!

## HOW TO GET STARTED!

 **Think now of an after-dark activity** for an upcoming troop meeting or campout. Use your imagination and come up with something the boys aren't expecting.

 **Think of some of your troop's** favorite daytime activities. Then see if they aren't something you can adapt to the dark. Hiking, compass courses, and canoeing are all activities that, when properly supervised, make exciting nighttime adventures.

 **Obtain a small notebook** to begin recording songs, stories, jokes, games, and other activities for campfires, or for times when you have an extra ten minutes to fill.

# 8

# EAGLE FEATHERS AND THE
# MACARONI MONSTER

## PUTTING THE FUN IN SERVICE

The troop had just returned from a short hike when thirteen-year-old Devin Black came bursting from his tent. His hands were full of dry macaroni.

"Hey!" he shouted. "Somebody's been in my tent! It's full of macaroni!"

A moment later a Scout named Clint poked his head from his tent.

"Mine too!" he shouted. "There's macaroni everywhere!"

In near panic, everyone dove for their tents where their worst fears were confirmed. There was macaroni in sleeping bags, macaroni in backpacks, macaroni in pockets, boots, socks, and in the occasional water bottle. One boy even found macaroni inside a bag of trail snacks.

As the boys were wondering what was going on, Parker and James—whose camping area was always neat as a pin—crawled from their tent. Each of them was holding a white feather.

"We didn't get any macaroni," James said. "But somebody left these on our sleeping bags."

Devin nodded knowingly.

"Ah," he said. "I think I get it . . . everyone but the Happy Homemakers gets macaroni. But the Happy Homemakers get feathers. I bet the macaroni is some sort of punishment."

Eager to test Devin's theory, the Scouts conducted a more thorough inspection of the campsite. Sure enough, each of the tents ambushed with macaroni was also in an advanced state of disaster. Most were so cluttered, it would have taken an extremely focused wizard from Hogwarts to sort them out.

Parker and James's tent was another story. Their packs were placed neatly inside the open tent flaps. Toothbrushes, compasses, and other articles were laid out in exact order, as if placed for a blind person. I even heard Devin muttering that the blades of grass beneath the tent were probably all bent in the same direction.

As it turned out, macaroni became a routine element of the troop's campouts. Even on weeklong excursions, the Scouts found macaroni in their tents any time they left them messy. And they found feathers whenever they left their gear orderly.

Eventually the Macaroni Monster began neglecting the younger Scouts, focusing his attention exclusively upon the troop's patrol leaders. His requirements were simple:

everyone in the patrol passed his surprise inspections, or the patrol leader returned to find his tent ambushed with macaroni.

"It was wonderful," Scoutmaster Jon Killpack told me. "For the first time, our patrol leaders began taking responsibility for their patrols. And I tell you, our campsites never looked better. Our boy leaders were far more demanding than I ever was."

In addition to improving the appearance of the troop campsite, Killpack said the Macaroni Monster taught his Scouts an important lesson. Cleaning camp was a chore; outwitting the Macaroni Monster was a game. The work was exactly the same, but the attitude was entirely different.

Work isn't much fun for most Scouts because it's, well, work! But many times, even the most hated and despised chores can be made tolerable, if not downright adventurous. All you have to do is add the element of challenge.

I once watched a troop clean up its campsite at the end of an overnighter. The Scouts were all tired and anxious to leave, and the idea of searching the campground one last time for overlooked bits of foil and litter didn't appeal to any of them. But then the senior patrol leader made an announcement.

"I spotted a certain piece of litter left on the ground somewhere," he said. "I have a candy bar for whoever brings it to me."

The next instant the boys were scouring the campsite, picking up every last bit of litter they could find. They weren't working because they were forced to. They were working because they wanted to . . . and they were doing a terrific job! They canvassed the area with the enthusiasm of hungry monkeys in search of bananas.

In a perfect world—and in a perfect troop—boys would do their chores and attack service projects with gusto and enthusiasm simply because they're Scouts and that's what Scouts are supposed to do. And many of them will for that very reason. But others of us need occasional pokes, prods, and nudges to keep us moving in the right direction, and teenage boys are no exception.

I know a Scoutmaster named Allen Keele who loves backpacking and who constantly drills his Scouts on no-trace camping techniques.

"Whenever you leave a campsite, you should never leave any sign that you've ever been there," he tells them, and he spends considerable time teaching the boys exactly how to accomplish that. And then on campouts, when it comes time to leave, he has his senior patrol leader inspect the camp for any trace of camping. If the boy can't find any, everyone gets milkshakes on the way home.

But if the youth leader does find something—even the tiniest bit of litter or charcoal from the fire—he is the only one to receive a reward.

"All it takes is one little bit of evidence," Keele told me. "A charred rock, a piece of litter, or a mark on a tree. And believe me, he looks hard . . . but the boys do so well that he rarely finds any thing. "

Camouflaging a campsite so completely and thoroughly isn't easy. But because Keele turned the chore into a game—making it a contest between the Scouts and their senior patrol leader—the boys put their best effort and enthusiasm into it.

When I was in college, I spent two weeks with my troop backpacking through Philmont Scout Ranch. And because we were camping in prime black bear country, each night we had to place all of our food and other "smellables" into a burlap bag that we hoisted into a convenient tree where it was safe from hungry, prowling bruins.

It was fun at first. But as the novelty wore off, so did the boys' enthusiasm for the assignment . . . especially when there wasn't any sign of bears. The boys moaned and groaned whenever it came their turn to gather the food and hang the bag, and I once found one dangling a mere ten feet off the ground and only twenty yards from camp.

But that all changed the night David Hillman took his turn. Feeling especially ambitious, he managed to haul the bag nearly fifty feet into the air.

Everybody laughed when they saw it.

"What are you protecting our stuff from, Dave?" someone asked. "Bigfoot on stilts?"

Dave just grinned.

"That's got to be some kind of record," he said proudly. "You might as well take a good look 'cause you'll never see a bear bag that high again."

And that's all it took. The next night, boys actually begged for the privilege of hanging the bear bag. It suddenly became a game to get it as high off the ground as possible. Scouts attacked the job enthusiastically every night—even those who weren't assigned to it—and when tall trees weren't conveniently located, it wasn't unusual for them to hang the bag eighty yards from camp. Only bears with extremely long legs or a knack for acrobatics could have possibly come close to stealing our breakfast. With a bit of creativity and a whole lot of enthusiasm, a tedious chore was suddenly a fun-filled adventure.

I remember once supervising a patrol of Scouts who had volunteered to clean the trash out of a stream below Camp

Maple Dell. Because of recent flooding, the streambed was full of rocks, logs, and other debris, which left little room for the fish. The boys spent a backbreaking hour sullenly throwing rocks out of the river, and it looked like they were in for several more when a Scout named Kenyon climbed onto a boulder and flexed his biceps.

"You guys are all wimps," he declared. "I bet I can throw rocks out of this river faster than any of you!"

Michael Davis sneered as he stood and stretched a kink from his back. "Yeah, right," he said. "Let's see you prove it!"

The boys climbed out of the stream and took seats on the bank, leaving Kenyon alone in the water. Michael held out his watch. "I'll give you one minute," he said as Kenyon searched for a spot with a lot of rocks. "Are you ready? Then . . . go!"

Kenyon bent over and began throwing rocks from the river as fast as he could. The boys on the bank counted each one as it flew through the air.

"One . . . two . . . three . . ."

Sixty seconds later, Michael yelled, "Stop!"

"Twenty-three rocks," a boy named Colby announced. "I can do better than that!"

And he did. Colby threw out twenty-seven rocks and Kenyon immediately demanded another turn. "Not until everyone's had a turn," Michael said, taking charge of the contest.

By the time everyone had taken a turn, Colby's record of twenty-seven rocks still stood, and Kenyon was fired up to beat him. Jumping back into the river, he stretched his arms and flexed his fingers.

"Okay," he said. "I'm throwing thirty rocks out of this

river or I'll buy everyone a candy bar!"

"Now you're talking," Michael said. "You've got a deal!"

Kenyon raised a finger. "But if I can do it, you all owe me one!"

"You're on!"

Kenyon began throwing rocks with the energy of a whirlwind. A minute later his thirty-second rock hit the bank.

"Yes!" he shouted, holding his hands over his head like an Olympic runner breaking the tape. "You can make that a Chocolate Crunchy, please."

Clearing the streambed wasn't the most exciting service project in the world. But as soon as it became a game, every boy's energy level went up like a bottle rocket, and everyone was suddenly anxious to participate. The work wasn't any different, but no one seemed to realize that. They went back to camp laughing and joking and reliving the experience, remembering the service project as an exciting adventure.

When your Scouts find fun in the work they do, they'll work harder, longer, and faster. They'll get more done, and they'll do it better than they otherwise would.

Not only that, but boys taught to look for the fun in their assignments will develop a healthy attitude toward work in general. They'll learn to cooperate with one another. They won't complain when there's work to be done.

Does any of this sound good? I'll bet it does. So try it! Look for ways to turn ordinary camp chores into contests. Find ways to turn work and service projects into challenges. Then see if your Scouts aren't a little more excited to participate.

I used to spend my summers working at Camp Maple

Dell. Most years, the camp staff is divided into patrols and assigned to take care of the general housekeeping chores that typically come up at camp. One patrol washes the dishes after dinner, for instance, as another cleans the bathrooms, one empties garbage cans, and another mops the floor of the camp lodge. None of it is much fun, of course. But I had a patrol leader one summer who knew how to make the most of unpleasant assignments. Any time we were washing dishes or mopping floors, for instance, he'd pop a tape of popular, upbeat music into a portable stereo and crank up the volume. The whole patrol sang, mopped, and rinsed in rhythm with the music, making the entire experience more endurable.

The work wasn't really any more fun (what *can* you do to make cleaning bathrooms exciting?), but it was at least more tolerable, and the time flew by much faster.

Another idea for keeping spirits high when the work is unpleasant is to take along a battery charger . . . you know, one of those people whose Grand Canyon–sized smile and firecracker personality is able to keep everyone happy, even when the day is cold and the work is hard.

When I was a Scout, my troop once volunteered to clean up an empty lot. It was a hot, sweltering day and dull, tiring work. But after we had been at it for half an hour or so, my friend Cannon suddenly arrived, screeching up on his bike and skidding to a stop.

"Helloooooooo, buckaroos!" he called, hopping off his bike and grinning like we were on our way to Disneyland. "I thought you guys would have this all done by now!"

Cannon apparently didn't understand that we were working, because he charged into the weeds like a teenage whirlwind. He picked up trash, pulled weeds, and hauled away rocks, all the time telling jokes and stories, laughing, and making everyone feel good. Within minutes I'd forgotten how tired I'd been feeling. In fact, I was actually having fun!

Another time when I was at Scout camp, I was asked to take a group of boys on a five-mile hike. It was raining that day, and I knew I'd be hearing a lot of moaning and groaning. So I took along a secret weapon: a boy named Tim.

Tim was thirteen years old, full of life and energy, and never without an ear-to-ear smile: he flashed his braces around like they were his most prized possession. From the moment we set out, slogging through the mud with rain dripping off the brims of our hats, Tim had us laughing and singing and feeling good.

What could have been a long, miserable hike was suddenly an adventure that still stands out as one of the highlights of the summer.

It would be nice if Scouts did their chores without being asked and attacked service projects with the enthusiasm of bottle rockets. But when your next work project comes, chances are you're going to need to do a little motivating. So try turning the work into a game. Give the work the element of challenge. And don't be afraid to take along a special "battery charger" or two.

As you do, the work will lose its unpleasantness. The boys will begin to find the joy in work well done, and you will have done them—and yourself!—a great service.

## HOW TO GET STARTED!

 **Find some incentive** for the next service project you do. Find some way to turn the work into a game or a challenge.

**Be sure to invite along a battery charger** to help keep everyone's spirits high as they work. It's great when this battery charger is another boy, but adults—or even younger boys—work well too.

 **Always be on the lookout for boys** who do their work without moaning or complaining. Find some way to show your appreciation for their good attitude. (At the same time, be on the lookout for those boys who might be helping the other boys.) These boys won't be looking for rewards or recognition, but let them know that they're making a difference.

# 9

## SNOWSHOES, SNOW CAVES, AND
# CARDBOARD
# CAMPOUTS

### PUTTING THE FUN IN WINTER

**C**annon Peterson huddled as close to the struggling campfire as he could get without setting fire to his coat or
gloves. His frozen breath hung in front of his face like
miniature clouds before wisping away in the dark, frosty
air.

"I've never been so cold in my life!" he said, stamping
his boots in the snow and wrapping his arms around himself.

"You're not half as cold as I am," I mumbled through
chattering teeth.

Cannon beat his arms against his chest. "Oh, no? Did
you sleep last night?"

"Yeah. . . . A little bit."

"Well, that settles it then!" he said. "I was too cold to sleep!"

It was so cold, I thought, that it could have frozen the whiskers off a polar bear. The night sky was as clear as a bell, and even in our snow caves, the temperature had plunged to miserable depths. By 4:30 a.m. everyone in the troop had crawled from their caves to huddle around Cannon's struggling fire.

I was just twelve years old at the time, and we were taking part in a Klondike Derby at Camp Maple Dell.

Klondike Derby?

It was so cold we were all referring to it as the "Frostbite Derby."

Andy Roberts held his hands over the fire. "I haven't been this cold since Jon and I went ice fishing and my toes nearly froze off."

Cannon looked around. "Where *is* Jon?"

No one knew.

Andy blew on his hands and shrugged. "I'll go find him."

He trudged off through the snow in the direction of Jon's snow cave, returning a few minutes later wearing an expression of profound envy.

"He's still in bed!" he reported. "He said he's too warm to get up!"

Everyone stared in disbelief.

"He's too warm?" someone asked through rattling teeth. "How can he be too warm?"

"I know!" Cannon agreed. "I'm so cold I don't think I'll ever be warm again!"

"He can't be that warm," a boy named Wyatt declared. "I'll go get him."

Wyatt disappeared into the darkness, returning a moment later wearing a look of triumph.

"He didn't want to get up," he said. "So I had to convince him."

"How did you do that?" I asked, knowing how stubborn Jon could be.

"Easy," Wyatt said with a mischievous grin. "I smashed in his snow cave!"

With the possible exceptions of The Three Bs—blisters, bad food, and Bigfoot—there's nothing that can make a Scout's experience of the outdoors more miserable than being cold. After all, there's just not much fun in having one's fingers freezing solid and dropping off.

But winter is one of the best times of the year to experience Scouting. It's a time of unparalleled beauty in the backcountry, and it provides opportunities and experiences unavailable during the warmer months. Many Scouts even rank snow activities among the highlights of the year. I've seen boys dig snow caves with such enthusiasm that their icy shelters became caverns capable of housing entire regiments of freezing Cossacks, only to spend the entire night skiing, rollicking, and throwing snowballs.

A Scoutmaster named Robert Newitt told me that his troop's favorite campout of the year takes place in the winter.

"We call it our Cardboard Campout," he told me. "And it's the one time of the year when we change all the rules."

Newitt explained that the troop begins by collecting large, cardboard packing boxes that they haul to the campsite. The Scouts then duct-tape the boxes together and cut doorways between them to form a miniature cardboard condominium. They complete their makeshift lodge by furnishing it with carpet, foam mattresses, and other amenities.

"We've reached the point that many of the boys even bring posters to hang on the walls," he said.

If the thought of such a cozy, comfortable campout bothers you, don't finish reading this paragraph. Newitt said that they always conduct their Cardboard Campout in places where they have access to electricity. Then, with the help of extension cords, they hook up a TV and DVD player and spend the night watching movies and eating popcorn.

"It's such an unusual, off-the-wall sort of activity that most boys wouldn't miss it for the world," he said. "We get a lot of boys out who normally don't like camping. . . . For us, it really is the highlight of the year."

My own troop developed such a love of cross-country skiing that after several trips on rented equipment, many of the boys bought their own. I lived in a home with a large backyard at the time, and the boys often brought their skis over to race through the apple trees. Just to make things a little more interesting, we once even set up an obstacle course in the trees for everyone to ski through.

Yes, winter activities can be exciting. But rest assured that not one of your boys will have any fun unless he's able to stay reasonably warm. So your first challenge in making cold-weather events fun is keeping the Scouts from getting cold. You'll need to make certain that they dress properly and have extra dry clothes to wear. And if you're going to spend the night, you'll need to make sure that they have tents and sleeping bags that are suitable for a night in the snow.

These things cannot be overemphasized. Going into the mountains unprepared is not only dangerous, but it can also dampen a Scout's enthusiasm for the outdoors. I know one young man, for instance, who faithfully attends all of his troop's activities . . . except campouts. His one—and only—camping experience was so miserable that he simply refuses to give it another try.

So when you plan a winter activity, remember that even well-prepared Scouts can get cold. And once they do, they'll stop having fun in a hurry. One remedy is to keep a large, warm-up fire going all the time. Assign one of your assistants to keep an eye on it. Then, whenever a boy's hands or feet get wet or cold, he can leave the fun long enough to warm his hands or dry his boots.

And if you really want to be the hero of the camp, keep a jug of hot chocolate ready. It might seem like a small pick-me-up, but a rich cup of steaming chocolate is often all it takes to rejuvenate a shivering Scout or spark life back into a frozen, miserable Scoutsicle. After a few minutes next to the fire and a cup of warm, marshmallow-topped chocolate, even the coldest Scouts will be ready to ski faster than a speeding Sasquatch and leap tall igloos in a single bound.

Many boys have limited experience in cold-weather camping, so it's an area where you might want to spend a little extra time in training. Before spending a snowy night in the backcountry, for instance, consider a "practice" campout behind the church building or in someone's backyard. (Knowing that they're close to home will help to alleviate the fear of sub-freezing camping for the more timid boys.) And be sure to emphasize the following tips to ensure a toasty (okay . . . at least a more comfortable) evening:

## NEVER GO TO BED WEARING WET CLOTHING
The best way to stay warm is to start warm. And to start dry. Most experienced Scouts, in fact, will take along socks, pants, an extra shirt, and a wool cap just for wearing to bed. No other tip will go further in ensuring that your Scouts spend a comfortable night than making cer-

tain they're wearing clean, dry clothes.

## PLACE AS MANY LAYERS BELOW THE SLEEPING BAG AS ABOVE

Inexperienced Scouts typically pile all of their extra blankets over their sleeping bags, forgetting that they need to be equally protected from the frozen ground below. Also remember that thin, closed-cell pads are more effective in insulating a sleeping camper than thick, spongy foam pads or air mattresses, which are designed to cushion rather than insulate.

So instruct your Scouts to bring a thick blanket or two to place beneath their sleeping bag in addition to the ones they're planning to place on top.

## DON'T ZIP THE TENT ALL THE WAY TO THE TOP

This seems to defy reason, allowing cold air inside the tent like that. But Scouts who crack the tent door four or five inches—and who open the windows just a bit—will sleep more comfortably than boys who have their tents zipped up tight. That's because a little circulation will prevent the buildup of frost inside.

Along those same lines, teach the boys to avoid the temptation to curl up—head and all—inside their sleeping bags. A typical camper will exhale a pint or more of moisture during the night, which can condense inside their sleeping bag, not only making them wet, but cold.

A better idea is to sleep with their head outside the bag, maintaining warmth by wearing a wool cap—or even a knit face mask—to bed. This will not only keep their head warm, but it will also help to conserve body heat during the night.

## PROTECT ALL OF THE NEXT DAY'S CLOTHING

Before going to bed, be sure that everything is put away so that it doesn't get covered with snow during the night. And to keep boots from freezing (I certainly hope that we're talking about boots and not tennis shoes here!), place them in the stuff sack of the tent or sleeping bag (turn the sacks inside out if the boots are muddy). Then place them at the foot of the sleeping bag, between the bag and the insulating pad.

## TOSS AN EXTRA DAB OF BUTTER INTO THE STEW AT DINNER TIME

A little extra butter will help to fuel the boys' inner furnace during the night. High-calorie snacks such as cheese, salami, and nuts before bedtime will also help to keep the boys warm during the night.

Keeping the boys warm is the first step in making winter activities more fun, and the next thing is to find activities that fire up the boys' imagination and spark their energy levels. One way to create exciting cold-weather activities is to take ordinary Scout skills and give them a winter flavor. How about an obstacle course in the snow, for instance? (And if you really want to make it fun, have the boys bring sleds or tubes. Hitch them up like a team of Huskies and send them through the course towing their patrol leaders.)

Or fire-building? Building a fire in four feet of snow is far different than building one in summer. And if you really want to test the boys' skills, take your troop into the woods, give them a pot and a couple of matches, and say, "Let's see how fast you can get a quart of water to boil." Building a fire from scratch in the snow—and collecting enough snow for a quart of water—will truly test their skills, not to mention their ability to work as a team.

Or astronomy? The stars and constellations visible during the winter months are entirely different than the ones you learn to identify in summer. I used to be part of an overnight cross-country ski adventure in Southern Utah. One of the things I most looked forward to each season was skiing beneath the canopy of winter stars. After skiing beneath them countless times, I came to look upon them as friends, and I missed them during the summer.

I know of one troop who waited until winter to teach boys to recognize and treat cold-weather hazards such as hypothermia, windburn, snowblindness, frostbite, and dehydration. They made certain everyone knew the signs and symptoms of each injury, as well as the correct prevention and treatment.

A similar idea is to practice winter rescue techniques, such as saving someone who has fallen through thin ice. Have a volunteer lay in the snow about twenty feet from the "shore." Then have the rest of the patrol race to tie several lengths of rope together and toss it to the "victim" before pulling him to "shore." (For a little added adventure, allow the victim to sit on an inner tube.)

When I was a Scout, the local chapter of the Order of the Arrow hosted an overnight snowshoe trek each January. And for me it was the highlight of the year. We used chapter dues to rent enough snowshoes for everyone and then trekked through the snow to a cave behind Mt. Timpanogas, where we spent the night. To this day, that snowshoe trek remains my fondest memory of the Order of the Arrow (and my greatest motivation for paying my dues).

Scoutmaster Shawn Rogers spends many of his winter troop meetings teaching his Scouts to make their own winter gear. They make their own snowshoes (just spend a few minutes on Google for hints and plans), and then they go on to make snow goggles and ice awls. Last on the list—and the most fun of all—is building a sled for the annual Klondike Derby.

My own troop once created a miniature golf course by stamping down links in the snow and using empty tuna fish cans as cups. Other fun activities include snow-sculpture contests, snowman-building contests (see who can make a snowman that most resembles the ward bishop, the troop Scoutmaster, or a favorite teacher at school), snowball-rolling contests (see who can roll the biggest snowball in five minutes), and ice-carving contests (freeze blocks of water in old milk cartons and then carve away!).

Because winter takes up such a major portion of the year, winter activities should take up a proportionate chunk of your Scouting calendar. And like most other things, winter activities are only limited by your imagination. So just because it's cold out there, don't believe that it's miserable. If you're properly dressed—and if you've got plenty of hot chocolate available—winter can provide some of your most successful activities of the year.

## HOW TO GET STARTED!

 **Take a minute right now** to jot down a few winter activities that your troop might enjoy. Even if it's summer, fire up your imagination and start listing ideas now so that you have plenty to choose from by the time colder weather arrives.

 **If your troop doesn't have a tradition** of winter activities—or if you have boys who aren't fond of the cold—begin your cold-weather curriculum with simple after-school activities such as snowball-rolling contests or mock ice-rescue games. Save the more elaborate overnighters for when the boys are truly ready for them.

If you have a winter campout coming up, plan a "practice" campout a couple of weeks earlier. Camp out behind the church, in a nearby park, or behind someone's house to build the boys' confidence. Then, while you're out, take a good, hard look at the boys' tents, sleeping bags, and clothing. Be certain the boys are all properly prepared for a real overnighter in the wilderness.

 Think of some of your troop's favorite activities: capture-the-flag, orienteering, fire building, first aid, astronomy, or whatever. Then see if you can't adapt any of them to winter. Find ways to enrich and expand favorite activities in a new environment.

 Remember that activities such as snowshoeing, cross-country skiing, building igloos and snow caves, ice fishing, and ice skating are only possible during the winter. Take advantage of them! Do as many winter activities as you can.

# CONCLUSION

# BOY SCOUTS TO THE
# RESCUE!

## COMING IN FROM THE FOG

**G**ood morning, Scouts!"

More than four hundred Boy Scouts and their leaders thundered back at the top of their lungs, "Good morning, Shane!"

Wow. . . . Standing in front of a camp full of Scouts and hearing them yell "good morning!" to me every day: that was one of the best things about working at Scout camp. Believe me, it never got old!

I love Scouting. It's changed my life and blessed me in more ways than I could ever describe. In this book I've shared a few of the things I've learned along the way, and I've shared a few of my favorite stories. I actually have a lot more, but my editor reminded me of something called "page count" and told me it was time to wrap things up.

Well, one more . . . one you might have heard before.

It was 1909, and American publisher William D. Boyce was in London on business. He became lost in a soupy English fog, and as he stood wondering what to do, a boy in uniform appeared from the gloom.

"May I help you find your way, sir?"

He could indeed! The boy took Boyce where he needed

to go. And then surprised the businessman by refusing to accept a tip.

"I'm a Scout," the boy explained. "I'm simply doing a good turn."

Intrigued, Boyce asked what a "Scout" was. He was so taken with the explanation that he asked his young friend to take him to the local Scout headquarters. And there he met the man—the founder of Scouting—Robert Baden-Powell.

And the rest is history. Boyce brought Scouting to the United States where it's become one of the largest youth organizations in the country. It's become the activity arm of the Aaronic Priesthood. It's affected millions of people . . . not only those who have participated as young men or adult leaders, but those who have been served—like Boyce—by Scouts going about their business. Scouting has turned boys into men, developed exceptional leaders, and instilled character, integrity, and direction in millions upon millions of young men.

And—not incidentally—it's the reason you're reading this book!

But the point I want to make is this: I don't believe that young boy in the fog ever knew what a difference he'd made. I don't believe he ever realized what an impact he'd had. I think he would be astounded to know that his simple act of service has affected so many millions of people . . . and that it's still affecting people today, more than a hundred years later.

Believe it or not, your efforts in Scouting will make a difference too. You may see some of the results of your work. I hope you do. But chances are you'll never know how much of a difference you've really made.

I recently received an email from a young man who'd

once been one of "my" Scouts. He's now the Young Men President of his stake, and he attached to his message a picture of all the Scouts in his stake—and their adult leaders—all in perfect Scout uniforms, poised like sailors on the deck of a ship returning proudly to port.

"You got me started in all this," he wrote, "and now look at me."

Wow.

I never had any idea.

And chances are, neither will you. But make no mistake: your work in Scouting will make a difference. It will bless the lives of others—not only those you actually teach and hike and cook and camp with, but those whom your Scouts will help and serve and bless along the way, and for the rest of their lives

Always remember that boy in the London fog. He once had a Scout leader just like you—a leader who made a difference. It's your turn now, so what are you waiting for?

Get up, get out, and get to work!

And have an absolute blast while you're doing it!

# ABOUT THE
# AUTHOR

In addition to many years' experience as a Scoutmaster, Shane Barker has served as program director at Boy Scout Camp Maple Dell, the Beaver High Adventure Base, the Scofield Aquatics Base, Adventure Park, and Cub Scout Camp Jeremiah Johnson. He has served on the faculty of the National Camping School and in a variety of district scouting positions.

Shane has written articles for *Boys' Life* and *Exploring* magazines, and he authored several books for teenage readers, including *Youth Leading Youth*; *Magnifying Your Aaronic Priesthood Calling*; *Even the Prophet Started out as a Deacon*; and *Stepping Up, Taking Charge, and Leading the Way*.

Shane is a popular speaker at Scout courts of honor and firesides. He is an avid skier and snowboarder and is an active member of the National Ski Patrol.

0  26575 55249  2